Origami for Kids

A Simple step-by-step Origami Guide for Beginners with over 30 Amazing Creative paper Lovely Projects with Animals, Flowers, Airplanes and Much More + Funny Origami Games

Copyright © 2019
Joel Kit & John Dover
All rights reserved.

TABLE OF CONTENTS

INTRODUCTION 5
   What is Origami? 5

CHAPTER 1: ANIMALS 6
   Jack the Bunny 7
   Swallow 11
   Sandy the Turtle 13
   Rico the Cat 17
   Penny the Puppy 19
   Lucas the Fish 21
   The Swan 23
   Bill the Pig 27

CHAPTER 2: FLOWERS 29
   The Tulipan 30
   5 Petal flower 33
   Cherry Blossom 35
   Rose 39
   Kawasaki Rose (medium level) 43

CHAPTER 3: AIRPLANES 51
   The simplest Airplane 52
   Air fighter 54
   High performance airplane 56
   Airplane with landing gear 58
   Swallow paper airplane 61
   Circular glider 64

CHAPTER 4: THE BEST ORIGAMI 66
   Cootie catcher 67
   Snowflake 69

Cute origami Santa 73

Easy leaves 77

Star boxes 80

Easy fish 83

CHAPTER 5: FUNNY ORIGAMI GAMES 87

Fortune teller 88

Jumping frog 90

Paper airplane 92

Paper basketball 93

Paper football 95

American paper football 96

Final Words 98

INTRODUCTION

What is Origami?

Origami is a very beautiful craft, perfect for all ages especially young children. Since Origami is quite easy to do with good instructions, it is the ideal activity for children to do to keep themselves busy. Brought to us by China, Origami became a craft many people of all ages began to do; since it is very easy yet so enjoyable. Within this book, you can learn how to do many different types of Origami...

If you want to create some Origami flowers, an Origami Plane or maybe you fancy doing the famous Origami swan. Whatever type of Origami you are interested in learning how to craft you can learn how to do that in this book!

Families with young children often struggle to find activities to do with their children, most things are either quite expensive or too time consuming. Origami is perfect for families with young children, quick, easy and fun. Just find the type of Origami you are interested in learning in the Table of Contents and follow the step-by-step instructions.

Ready to begin folding? Then let's begin...

CHAPTER 1: ANIMALS

Origami Animals are definitely one of the most fun types of Origami to craft! Young kids and families will enjoy folding the animals in this chapter, all of the animals are fairly easy to fold with a few exceptions of course. Kids can have a lot of fun with Origami Animals since there is a lot to do after the folding process is done. Such as, adding whiskers, facial features and colouring or painting the animal! Have fun learning how to fold these easy & cute Origami Animals...

Jack the Bunny

Everybody loves bunny rabbits, right? Well, if you do you are probably interested in an Origami bunny. Jack the bunny is a great piece of Origami, if you follow the step-by-step instructions below you will have your very own bunny. An Origami bunny is easy to fold and looks great once completed, perfect around Easter time. This project isn't just great for Easter, but if you are creating this bunny around Easter maybe add a bit of sparkle to your bunny. Without further-a-do let's get folding Jack the Bunny!

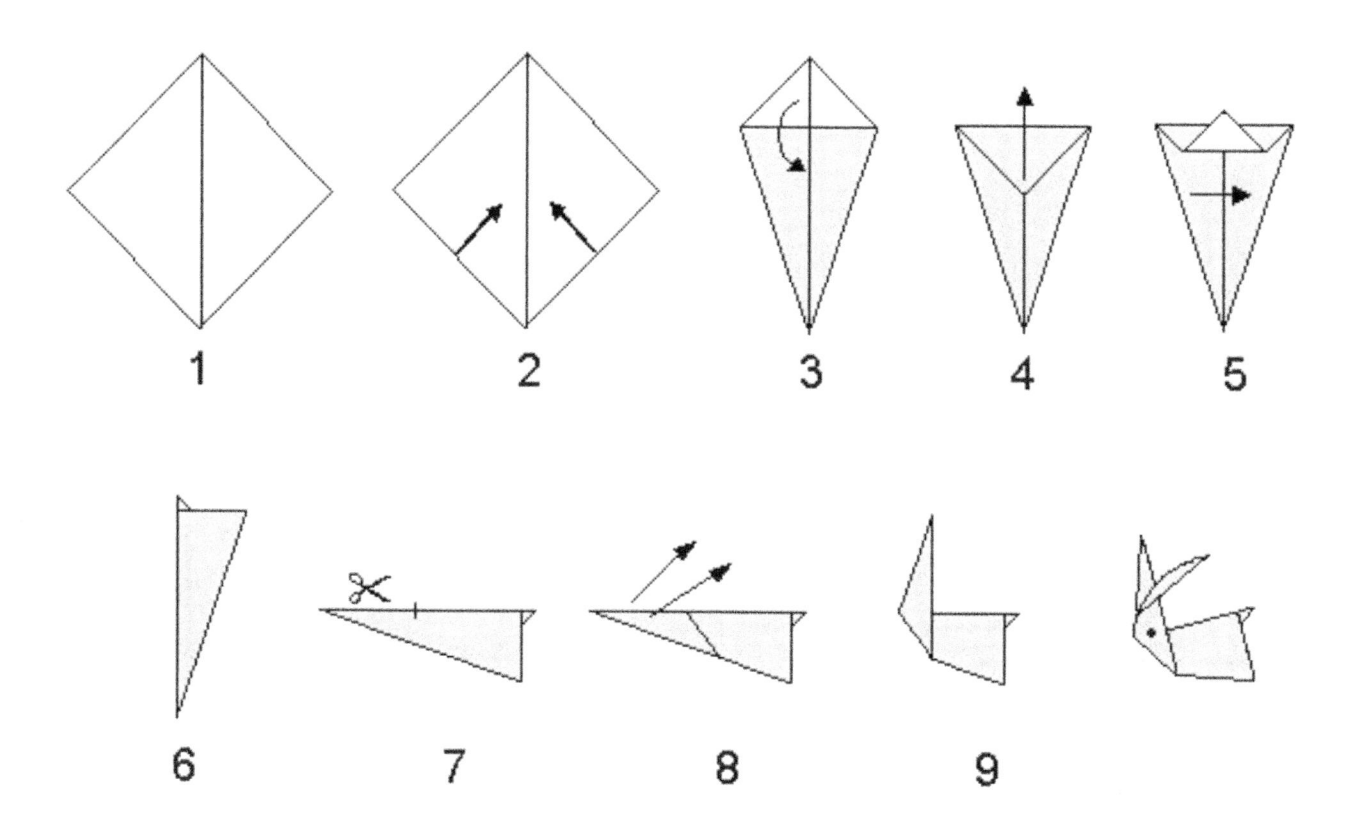

Jack the Bunny Step 1:

Begin by placing the colour side down, in other words make sure you cannot see the colour or pattern unless you want an odd bunny! You don't want that... Then fold the piece of paper in half diagonally to make a triangle.

Jack the Bunny Step 2:

Unfold the triangle back into a square, fold both sides to meet the crease. You should be left with a kite shape.

Jack the Bunny Step 3:

The next step is to fold the tip over to the left side, to overlap the "kite" body.

Jack the Bunny Step 4:

Grab the tip you just folded over to the left, which should now be a flap and about halfway up fold the flap back up. Or two thirds of the way up, follow the diagram above .

Jack the Bunny Step 5:

Turn the paper over onto the other side, now you need to cut from left to right. Please follow the image above. Cut a third of the way up or follow the line on the diagram.

Jack the Bunny Step 6:

Fold it in half, now fold up the left ends up for both sides of the paper - Fold the flaps up where you previously cut, you need to do this for both sides.

Jack the Bunny Step 7:

You should have your bunny now! However, if you want the best Origami bunny you should add some eyes, maybe a mouth and whiskers. Once that is done, you have your very first bunny! Well done.

You can create different size bunnies once you feel confident with folding this bunny! It can be very fun to see different coloured rabbits, small, big and it is definitely a good activity to pass time. At Easter time you can fold a larger bunny and paint it with different colours, this is a perfect activity for families or teachers to do with their class! If you want to add more detail to make your bunny stand out, colour the outline with a black marker...

Swallow

Swallows are found all around the world, on every single continent – including Antarctica on occasion Many people know what a swallow looks like, it has a very memorable appearance. Origami birds are mostly very difficult to do, but the swallow is actually quite easy to fold. The wings on Origami birds are the most difficult part of the process, however for the Swallow they are quite easy compared to other Origami birds. This piece of Origami is especially good for young children, folding this bird can be very fun for families or a class of young students. Furthermore, Origami birds can be used for decorations and the Swallow is definitely one of the best pieces of Origami for decorating. Perfect all around the year, why wouldn't you want to fold a swallow? Follow the instructions below to learn how to fold the extraordinary swallow!

Swallow Step 1:

Begin with a square piece of Origami paper, fold the paper in half from the top corner to the bottom corner. Then fold part of the top down so that the edge is about halfway down the paper. Don't let this flap too thin as this will become the wings.

Swallow Step 2:

Turn the paper over to the other side, take the bottom corner of the top layer and fold it up. Fold the paper in half by folding the left side over to the right.

Swallow Step 3:

Now fold the flap back to create the wing, then fold the other wing back as well.

Swallow Step 4:

Push the centre of the head in and flatten, the head is on the right side above the wings.

Swallow Step 5:

Now you have yourself a bird! Doesn't it look amazingly beautiful... Once you have folded your Swallow, you can paint it, colour it or add patterns to it to make it even more beautiful! If you did want to paint it, you need to use thicker paper so that the paper doesn't get to wet.

Sandy the Turtle

Turtles are very mysterious animals, but very beautiful at the same time. If you are ever lucky enough to see a turtle, you will see just how incredible turtles are. Folding a turtle is very fun for a family to do or a group of friends, especially when you get to compare your turtles. An Origami turtle is very simple to make, it also looks great upon completion. Therefore, why not learn how to fold an Origami turtle? There are plenty of ways to fold an Origami turtle, however the one below is by far the easiest to learn! If you want to make a great looking Origami Turtle then follow the step-by-step guide below – ready? Great! Let's begin...

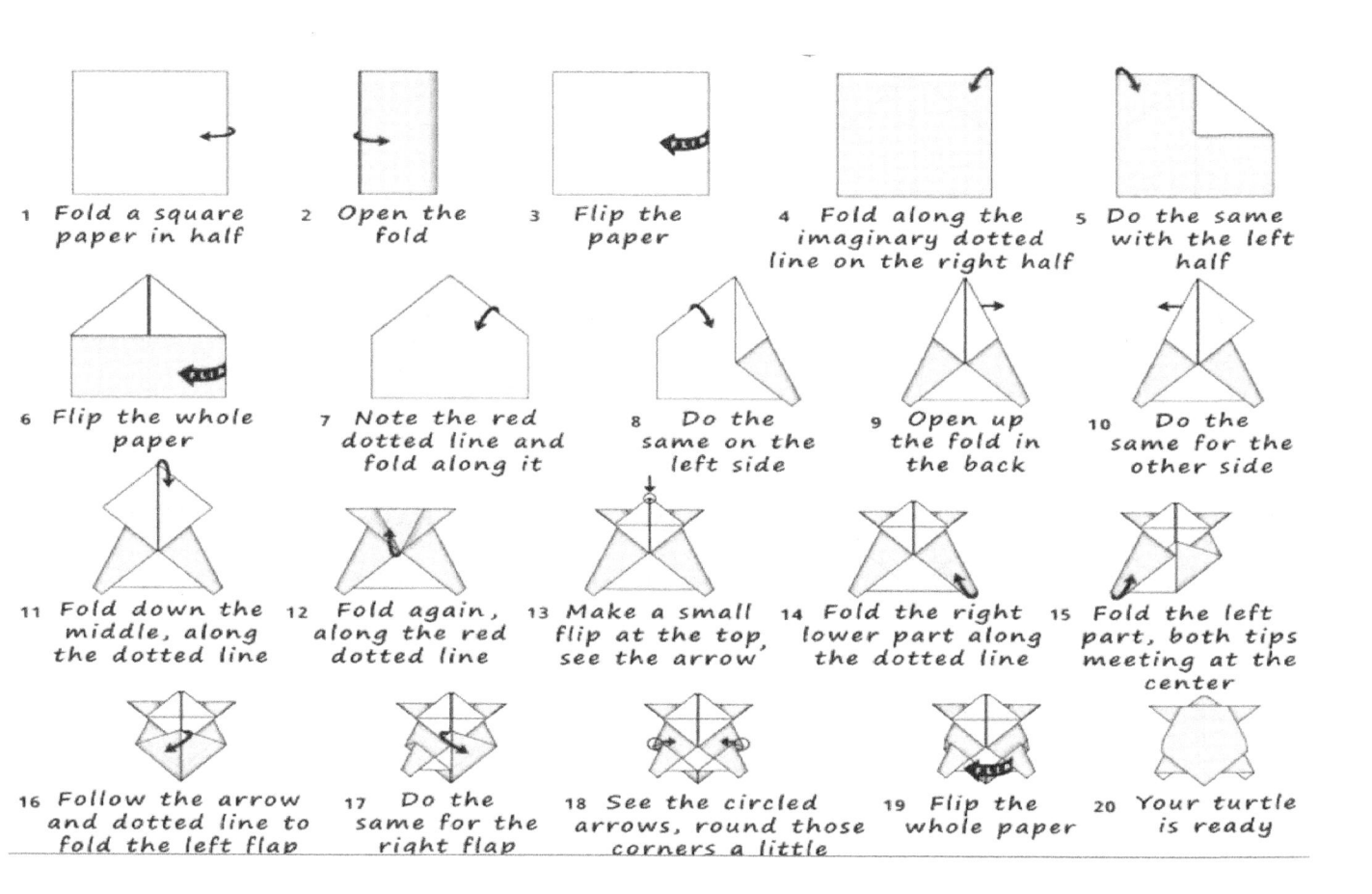

1. Fold a square paper in half
2. Open the fold
3. Flip the paper
4. Fold along the imaginary dotted line on the right half
5. Do the same with the left half
6. Flip the whole paper
7. Note the red dotted line and fold along it
8. Do the same on the left side
9. Open up the fold in the back
10. Do the same for the other side
11. Fold down the middle, along the dotted line
12. Fold again, along the red dotted line
13. Make a small flip at the top, see the arrow
14. Fold the right lower part along the dotted line
15. Fold the left part, both tips meeting at the center
16. Follow the arrow and dotted line to fold the left flap
17. Do the same for the right flap
18. See the circled arrows, round those corners a little
19. Flip the whole paper
20. Your turtle is ready

Sandy The Turtle Step 1:

Use an A4 size paper, it is best to use paper with colour on both sides for this piece of Origami.

Sandy The Turtle Step 2:

Fold your piece of paper in half vertically, fold your paper over to the right from the left to create a vertical fold. Make sure to run your figure down the crease once folded!

Sandy The Turtle Step 3:

Unfold the piece of paper and flip it over so that the crease is facing up.

Sandy The Turtle Step 4:

Fold the top corners of the paper in to meet the crease. The left and right corners should be brought in to align with the crease, these folds should be triangular. The diagram above shows what the folds should look like.

Sandy The Turtle Step 5:

Flip your paper back over to the original side, then fold both sides into the centre crease. The two flaps from underneath the paper need to be flipped up but not folded yet. You should be left with a diamond shape at the top of your paper.

Sandy The Turtle Step 6:

Tuck the points in at the bottom of your paper, tuck them above the bottom layer but below the top layer of the paper. This should make a straight bottom edge.

Sandy The Turtle Step 7:

Fold the top of the paper down in half, the diamond shape should be even with the small triangular area tip of the other half of the diamond. You should be folding towards yourself.

Sandy The Turtle Step 8:

Fold the top layer back over itself in half, the layer you just folded. Fold away from you. Run your finger over the fold to make it stay in place!

Sandy The Turtle Step 9:

Fold the bottom corners into the centre crease, the left and right corners at the bottom of your paper.

Sandy The Turtle Step 10:

Fold the two flaps you have just folded up down toward you, you want to fold 2/3 of the flaps. In other words, make sure more of the flap is pointing out towards you, the image below shows what this should look like.

Sandy The Turtle Step 11:

Flip the paper! You now have a turtle! If you haven't used green paper you can paint the turtle green. Wasn't that easy...

If you haven't used green paper, then colour your turtle or paint it to give it a better finish. Just be sure to not use too much paint or else the turtle will collapse! This turtle looks great as a decoration!

Rico the Cat

Kids will love to fold an Origami cat; it is a simple piece of Origami and also allows them to colour the cat's face. Cats are perfect for Origami, cute and very easy to do! An Origami cat must be one of the easiest pieces of Origami to do, kids are bound to enjoy folding this cat. Also, this can be a great activity for a family or a group of friends. This cat is very enjoyable to fold, follow the steps below to have your very own Origami cat in just a few minutes! Are you ready to make a cute little Origami cat? Perfect! Let's get folding...

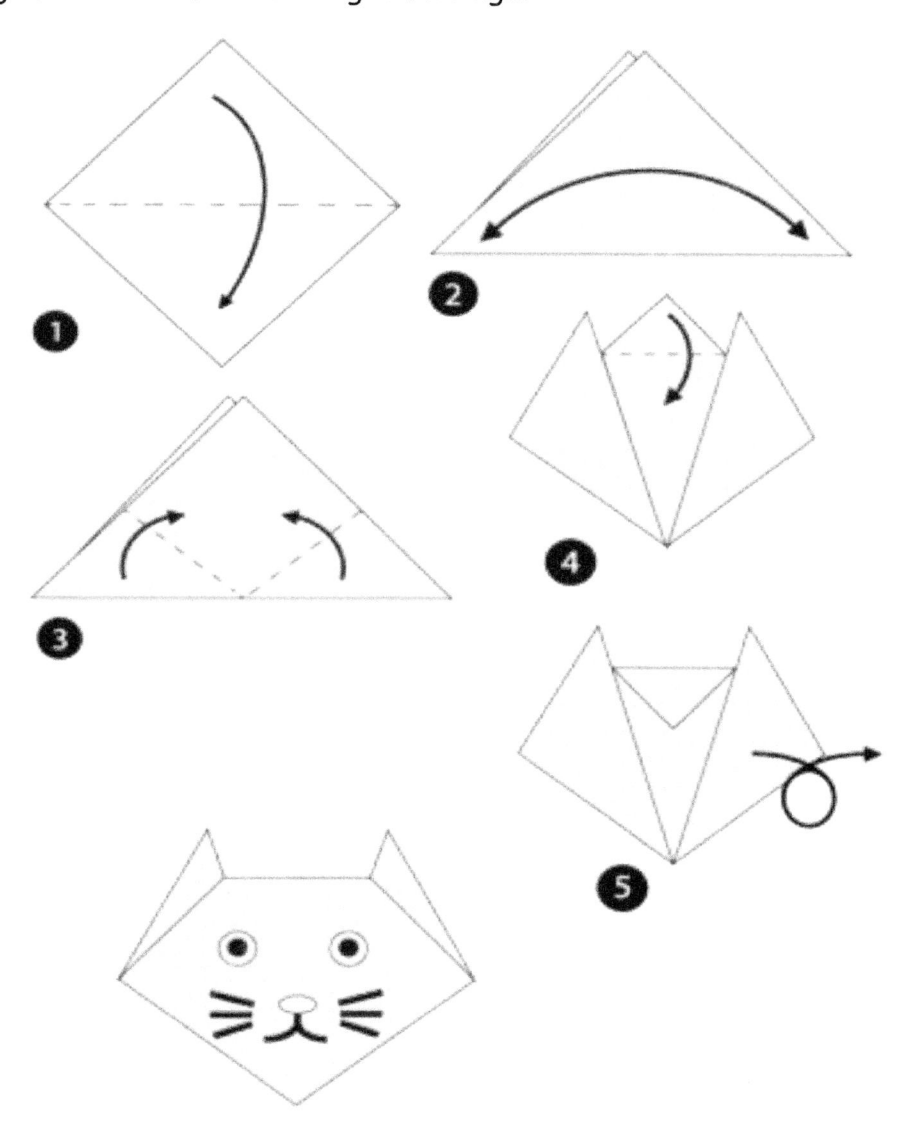

17

Rico The Cat Step 1:

Begin with a square piece of Origami paper and once again coloured on both sides is best. Fold the bottom corner to meet the top corner, a horizontal fold.

Rico The Cat Step 2:

Fold the left corner to meet the right corner, a vertical fold.

Rico The Cat Step 3:

To form the ears fold the left and right lower corners up at an angle, check the diagram above to see what result you should see.

Rico The Cat Step 4:

Fold the top corner down towards yourself, only fold to match the image.

Rico The Cat Step 5:

Turn the paper over, draw some eyes, whiskers and a nose! Once that is done you have a cat!

Penny the Puppy

Everybody loves dogs... Especially puppies! Well, wouldn't you like to be able to make your very own puppy? To keep as your pet, to show to family and friends or to show off in class at school! Or maybe you want someone to keep Rico the Cat company. If that is the case, then follow the step-by-step instructions below and you will have the most adorable Origami puppy below! An Origami puppy is one of the easiest Origami animals to make, perfect for kids to have fun with. One of the great things about an Origami puppy is that children can colour and add facial features once the puppy is folded. Are you ready to start folding your puppy? Then let's start folding!

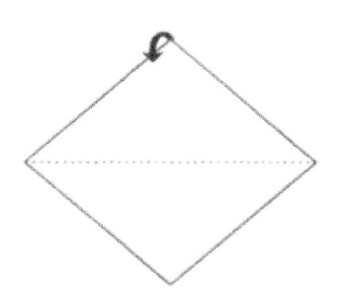

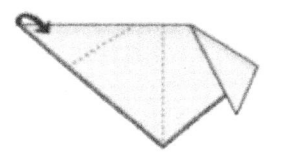

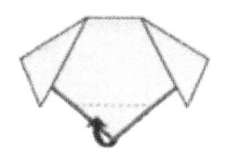

1. Fold a square piece of paper in half
2. Make creases at the center and the sides
3. Fold along the right dotted line
4. Repeat for the left side
5. Fold the lower tip up
6. Draw the eye and mouth
7. Fill them up in black

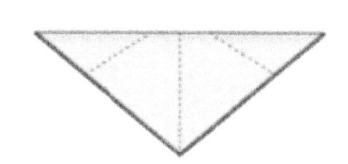

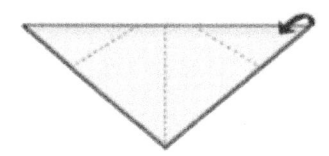

Penny The Puppy Step 3:

Unfold the vertical fold and then to form the ears fold the left and right upper corners down at an angle but leave a gap between the ears and the center crease.

Penny The Puppy Step 4:

Fold the bottom corner up over the paper, only fold to match the diagram.

Penny The Puppy Step 5:

Fold part of the corner you have just folded down towards yourself. This will act as the tongue!

Penny The Puppy Step 6:

All that is left to do is to add some eyes, a nose and colour the tongue! Now you have done that you have a puppy!

Lucas the Fish

Origami definitely is a beautiful craft but for sure one of the most beautiful types of Origami to fold are sea creatures. Why not learn how to fold one?! A simple Origami fish is perfect for kids, it is always fun to colour this fish afterwards add eyes and scales. Once you have learnt how to do this fish, you can fold many more to have a party of fish. You could even attempt to make a bigger fish with a bigger piece of paper for fun! Ready to learn how to make an Origami fish? Then let's fold this fish!

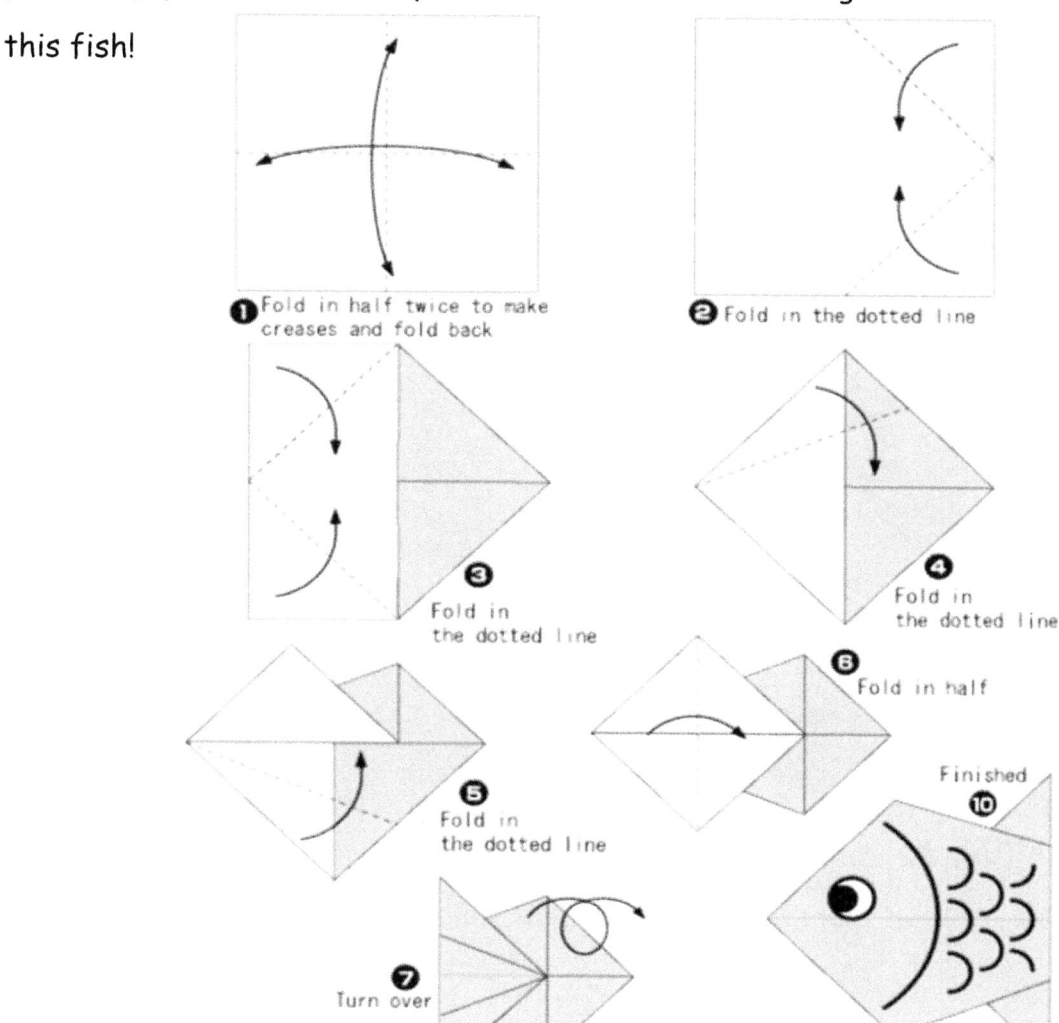

❶ Fold in half twice to make creases and fold back

❷ Fold in the dotted line

❸ Fold in the dotted line

❹ Fold in the dotted line

❺ Fold in the dotted line

❻ Fold in half

❼ Turn over

❿ Finished

A Basic Fish Step 1:

First begin by getting a square piece of Origami paper, fold it in half diagonally from corner to corner. Then unfold it and fold in half diagonally from the other corner to corner. Once again unfold.

A Basic Fish Step 2:

Fold in half horizontally, then unfold it and fold horizontally the other way. Once again unfold.

A Basic Fish Step 3:

Fold the bottom right corner to meet the centre crease, this should be a small triangle. Now fold the bottom left corner to meet the centre crease, this should also be a small triangle. Then flatten the flap which is left on top of those triangles. This will make a larger triangle!

A Basic Fish Step 4:

Fold the bottom left corner of the top larger triangle towards the centre crease, at a slight angle though. Then overlap the bottom right corner of the same triangle towards the centre crease over the top of the fold you just did.

A Basic Fish Step 5:

Flip over, now you have your fish! Add some eyes, colour it if you wish and have fun with it!

The Swan

Everybody must know about the Origami Swan... Well, surely you must have seen or heard about it at least once. Learning how to fold The Swan is actually quite simple and easy. Of course, swans are beautiful and being able to replicate the beauty of the swan through Origami is amazing! Swans are very elegant, beautiful and gracious animals. Floating down the river or floating on a lake, swans are always peaceful and calm. If you can fold such a beautiful animal it is quite an achievement and a great feeling once done! If you would like to learn how to fold an Origami swan then follow the instructions below, enjoy!

Origami Swan

The Swan Step 1:

Begin with a square piece of paper, white side facing up. Fold the paper in half diagonally and unfold.

The Swan Step 2:

Fold the left and right edges into the centre, make sure your paper is facing white side up like a diamond shape... Once the left and right edges have been folded into the centre you should be left with a kite shape. Flip the paper over.

The Swan Step 3:

Once again fold the left and right edges into the centre, now fold the bottom point up over to the top this should align with the top point. Fold down a small section of that fold to make the swans head.

The Swan Step 4:

Fold the paper in half, this will create the swan body, fold from left to right. Make sure to fold backwards, away from the swan head. Once that is done, fold the swans head back up.

The Swan Step 5:

Now that is done, you have a swan! You can add some eyes if you wish, maybe make a few more swans and make a small swan family!

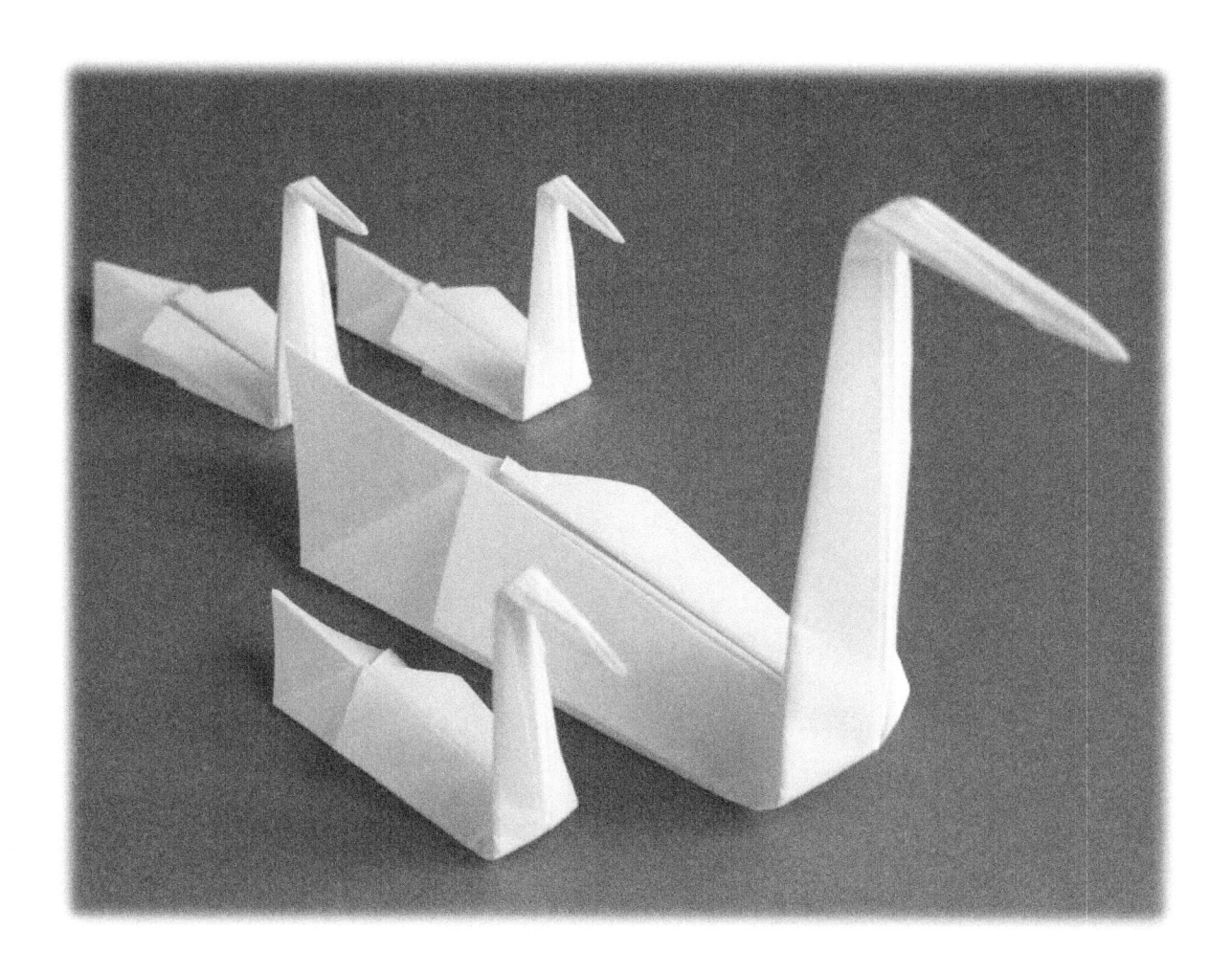

You can fold different size swans which you can than place all together as ornaments on windowsills, tables, mantlepieces or anywhere you want! They do make very good decorations... Well done for completing your swan!

Bill the Pig

Pigs are one of the simplest pieces of Origami to create, a great place for kids or beginners to start. The Origami pig is very fun to fold, sit down with family or friends and fold away! This pig face is very simple to do but looks great, if you want to fold a pig with a body you will have to learn how to fold a pig face first! There are many ways to fold an Origami pig, most are difficult to do... However, in this book everything is easy! So therefore, the step-by-step process below is very easy to follow but the result is very satisfying. Ready to fold your very own Origami pig?

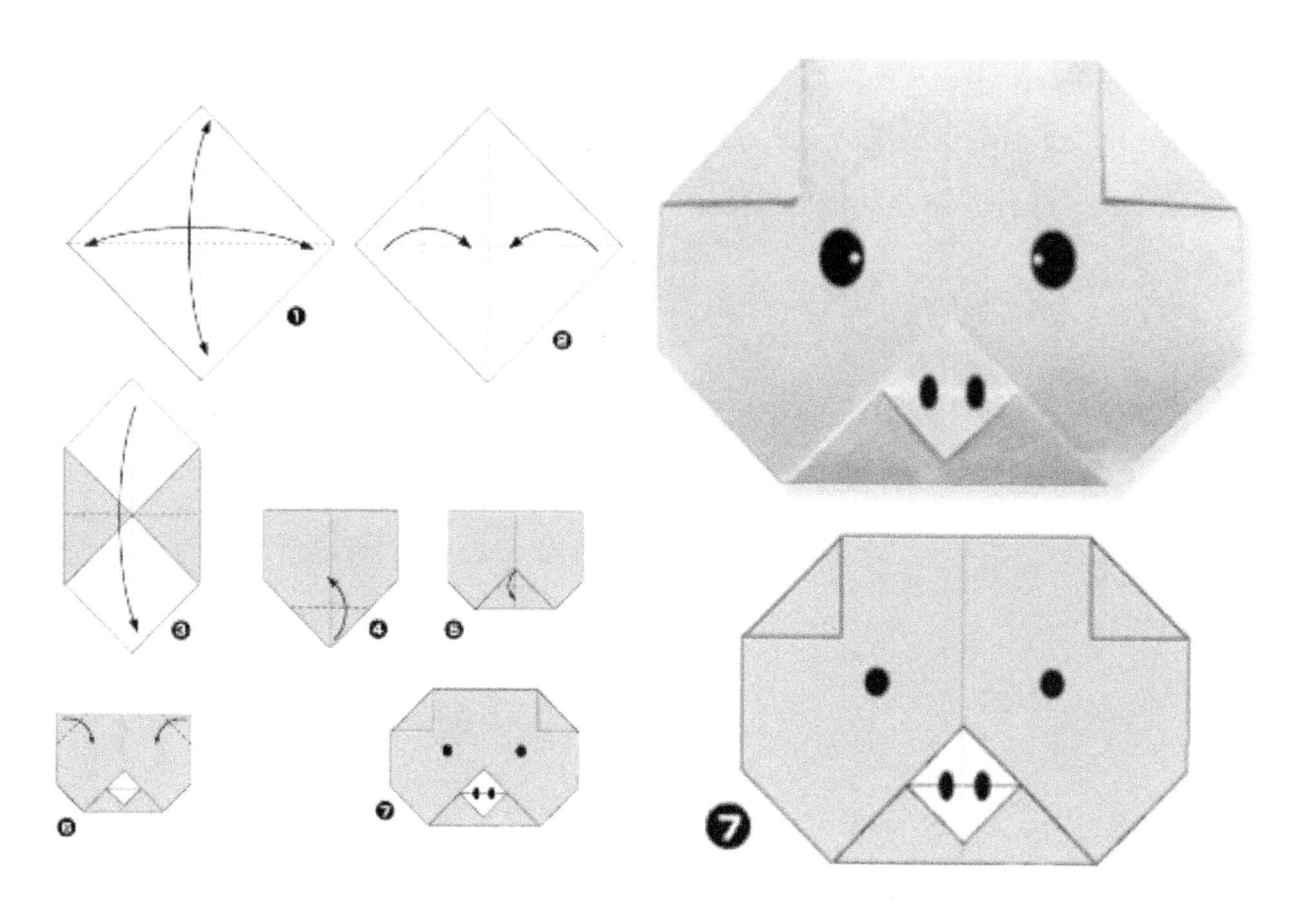

Bill The Pig Step 1:

Begin with a square piece of Origami paper, preferably colour on both sides. Fold the square in half diagonally, unfold and fold diagonally the other corner to corner.

Bill The Pig Step 2:

Fold 2 corners to meet in the centre of the paper, fold one corner into the centre and then fold the opposite corner into the centre to meet.

Bill The Pig Step 3:

Now you need to fold from top to bottom, along the centre crease line.

Bill The Pig Step 4:

To form the ears fold the left and right corners down. Bring the bottom point up and fold over, to from a snout fold down the point you have just folded in half again.

Bill The Pig Step 5:

You now have a pig! Add eyes and colour on the snout to have the best finish!

CHAPTER 2: FLOWERS

Origami Flowers are beautiful and can be easy, with the right instructions! Although you may need an adult/parent for help, some steps are difficult. Kids will definitely have a lot of fun folding these flowers, some of these are very hard but with an adult's help you will surely be able to fold all of the flowers in this chapter. There are many classic Origami flowers in this chapter, so have fun folding those! You may be wondering what are Origami flowers for? Well... You can give them out as gifts, use them as decorations, colour them, use for Christmas or Easter. There are many different ways to use Origami flowers! Ready to learn how to fold some Origami flowers?

The Tulipan

Flowers are perfect for Origami, beautiful, simple and very fun to make. The Tulipan sounds difficult, but it isn't! Tulips are very beautiful flowers, one of the most popular Origami flowers and it is so easy to fold! Origami Tulips are simple and can be folded quite quick, which is good for when you want to create a bunch of tulips. The steps below explain very easily how to fold a Tulip flower, just follow the step-by-step instructions and you will have a very pretty flower. Preferably use Origami paper with colour on both sides...

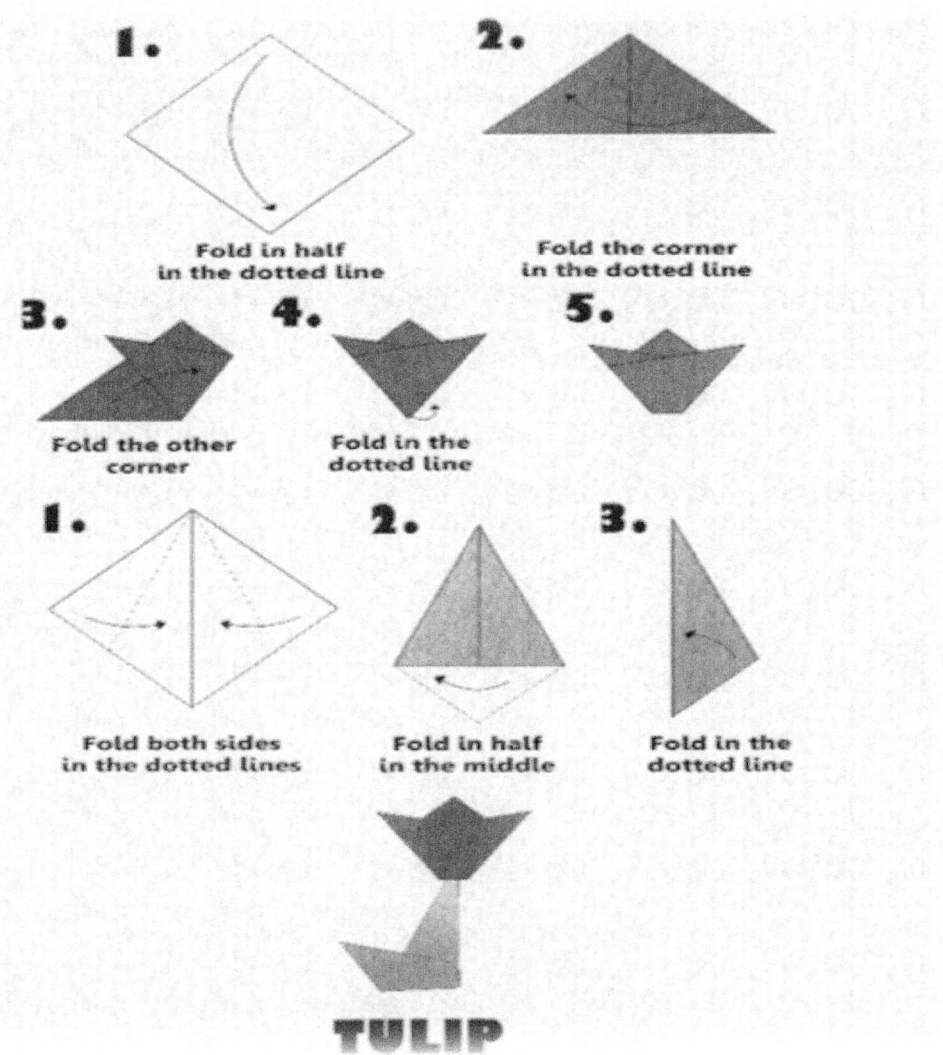

1. Fold in half in the dotted line

2. Fold the corner in the dotted line

3. Fold the other corner

4. Fold in the dotted line

5.

1. Fold both sides in the dotted lines

2. Fold in half in the middle

3. Fold in the dotted line

TULIP

The Tulipan Step 1:

Begin with a square piece of Origami paper, rotate it so that one point is pointing towards you and one point is pointing away. This should look like a diamond.

The Tulipan Step 2:

Fold in half from the bottom to the top, fold in half from left to right now. Unfold the last fold only.

The Tulipan Step 3:

Take the bottom right corner and fold it diagonally upwards across to the left, just like in the diagram. Do the same for the left corner, fold it over the top diagonally upwards across to the right.

The Tulipan Step 4:

Fold the bottom point behind the paper.

The Tulipan Step 5:

Take out a new sheet of square Origami paper for the stem. Once again have the paper laid out like a diamond. Fold the paper from left to right this time, from point to point.

The Tulipan Step 6:

Unfold it. Grab the left and right corners and fold them to the centre crease, this should create a kite shape.

The Tulipan Step 7:

Fold in half from left to right. Take the small portion at the bottom and fold it up towards the left. Glue or tape the tulip on top... Now your tulip is done!

Once your Origami Tulip is finished, you can fold a few more then stand them together which creates a nice bunch of tulips effect.

5 Petal flower

The 5-petal flower can be quite difficult to do, although if you follow the steps below it will be easier to do! Flowers can be tricky to do, but that is why they are much more fun to do... You will need help from parents, or you can try yourself, but the 5-petal flower can be hard to fold. This type of flower is very beautiful once completed though, if you can do this you will definitely have learnt how to fold one of the most stunning Origami Flowers... Ready to fold a 5-petal flower?

5 Petal Flower Step 1:

Begin by getting 5 pieces of Origami paper that are the same length. Fold one piece of paper in half diagonally from point to point. Fold the left corner into the centre, do the same with the right corner so they meet in the centre.

5 Petal Flower Step 2:

Fold the left and right corners down to meet the edge of your paper. Now flatten the flaps you have just created and fold the triangles down, look at the diagram for guidance.

5 Petal Flower Step 3:

Fold the left corner in so it meets the first side crease, repeat with the right corner. Glue your petal together carefully!

5 Petal Flower Step 4:

Repeat the previous steps for the next 4 sheets of Origami paper. Once that is done glue all your petals together... Well done! You have folded a 5-petal flower.

IF you wish to do an 8-petal flower, repeat all the steps 8 times... Now you know how to fold a 5-petal flower and an 8-petal flower! That is incredible.

Cherry Blossom

In Japan, cherry blossoms are called Sakura, a special flower for the people and the country. Cherry blossoms are a symbolic flower of the spring, a time of renewal, and the fleeting nature of life. ... Hanami literally means "watching blossoms," and the tradition can be traced back at least a thousand years. The Origami Cherry Blossom flower is quite challenging but looks beautiful once completed, but if you want to create Origami flowers then the Cherry Blossom is one of the most beautiful types. Once again you may need help from an adult... Are you ready to start folding your Cherry Blossom? Then let's begin, follow all the steps below...

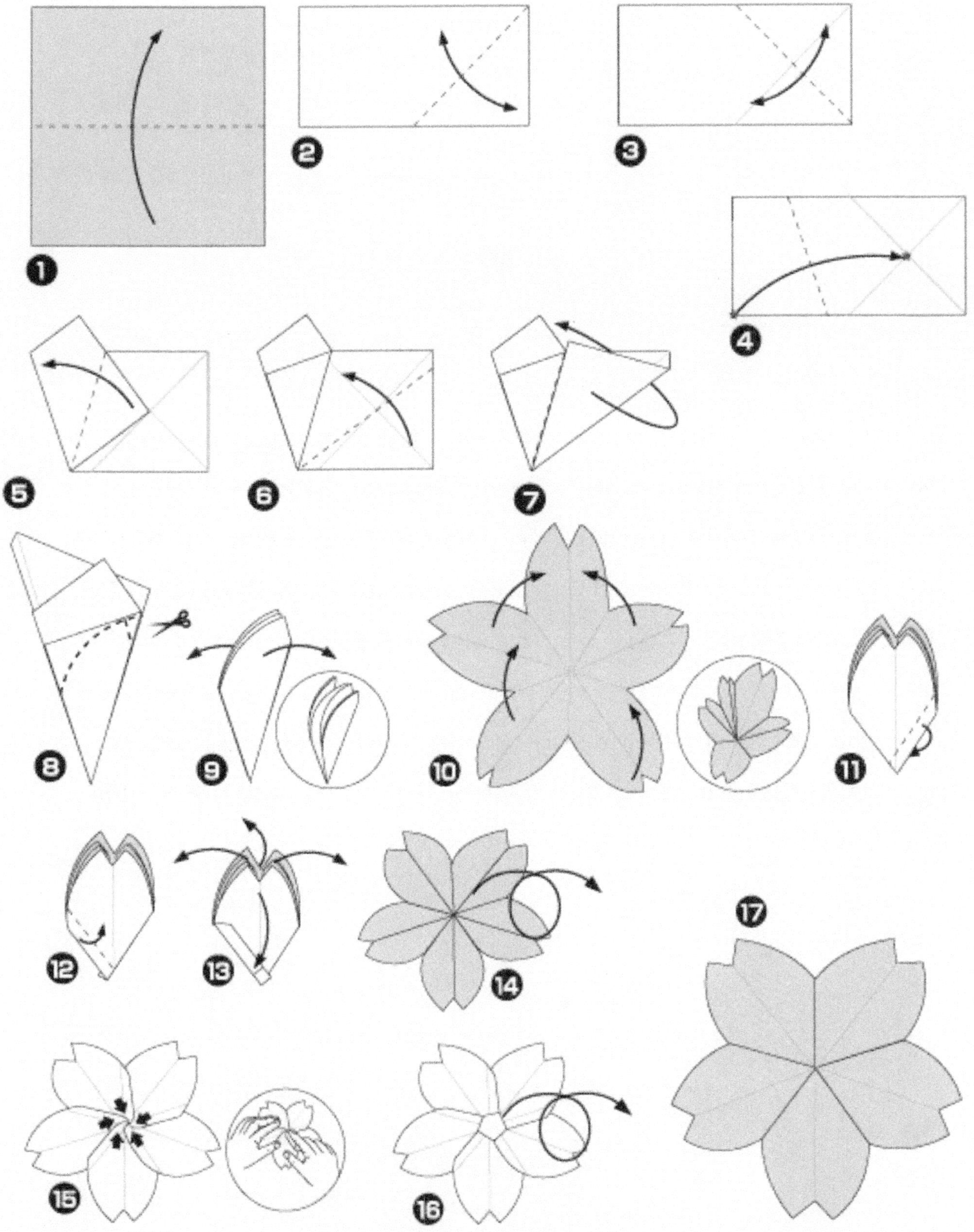
1
2
3
4
5
6
7
8
9
10
11
12
13
14
15
16
17

Cherry Blossom Step 1:

Fold the bottom of edge of your paper up to the top, now fold the bottom left corner towards the centre but only crease the middle point. Bring the top left corner down to the centre and crease the centre point only again. This should create an "X" marking the centre of the left side of the paper.

Cherry Blossom Step 2:

Bring the bottom right corner to the centre of the "X" and crease. Fold that flap over to the right, align it with the vertical edge of the right side.

Cherry Blossom Step 3:

Now, take the bottom left corner and fold it up to the right aligning it with the left vertical edge of the right side.

Cherry Blossom Step 4:

Next fold the entire left section behind, make sure top fold along the same vertical edge. Now cut the bottom point off to create a petal, you can cut the paper a different way to get a different petal each time.

Cherry Blossom Step 5:

Unfold the paper carefully, then re-fold the flower making each fold is a valley fold (V). Once that is done, fold the lower left edge inwards a little. Turn the paper over, fold the lower left edge inwards again the same amount as the previous fold.

Cherry Blossom Step 6:

Unfold the flower carefully, bring the petals from behind down. Then pull the top section out to the right and hold onto the little square at the same time lifting it slightly. Now flatten the flower, begin twisting the centre point in a clockwise motion.

Cherry Blossom Step 7:

Flatten out the centre gently, it should look like a small pentagon. Flip the paper over and you will have your cherry blossom flower!

If you want to make your Cherry Blossom that bit better... Colour each petal a difference colour which creates a very nice effect! Or make more than one cherry blossom colour each one a different colour then bunching them together to create a very nice mixed effect! You could even attempt to create a bigger Cherry Blossom using a bigger size paper, it will be harder to fold but very fun... Not only that but it will look great to have a big Cherry Blossom as a decoration around your house! Have fun...

Rose

Roses are very beautiful flowers, often used for romance or to show love. Origami Roses are amongst the most popular Origami projects, many Origami roses are far too hard for children. Roses are a very beautiful flower but very hard for children or beginners to learn. This Origami rose is simple enough for children to fold, although they may struggle with smaller folds. For the smaller folds ask an adult for help! For this piece of Origami, you will need Origami paper with colour on both sides.

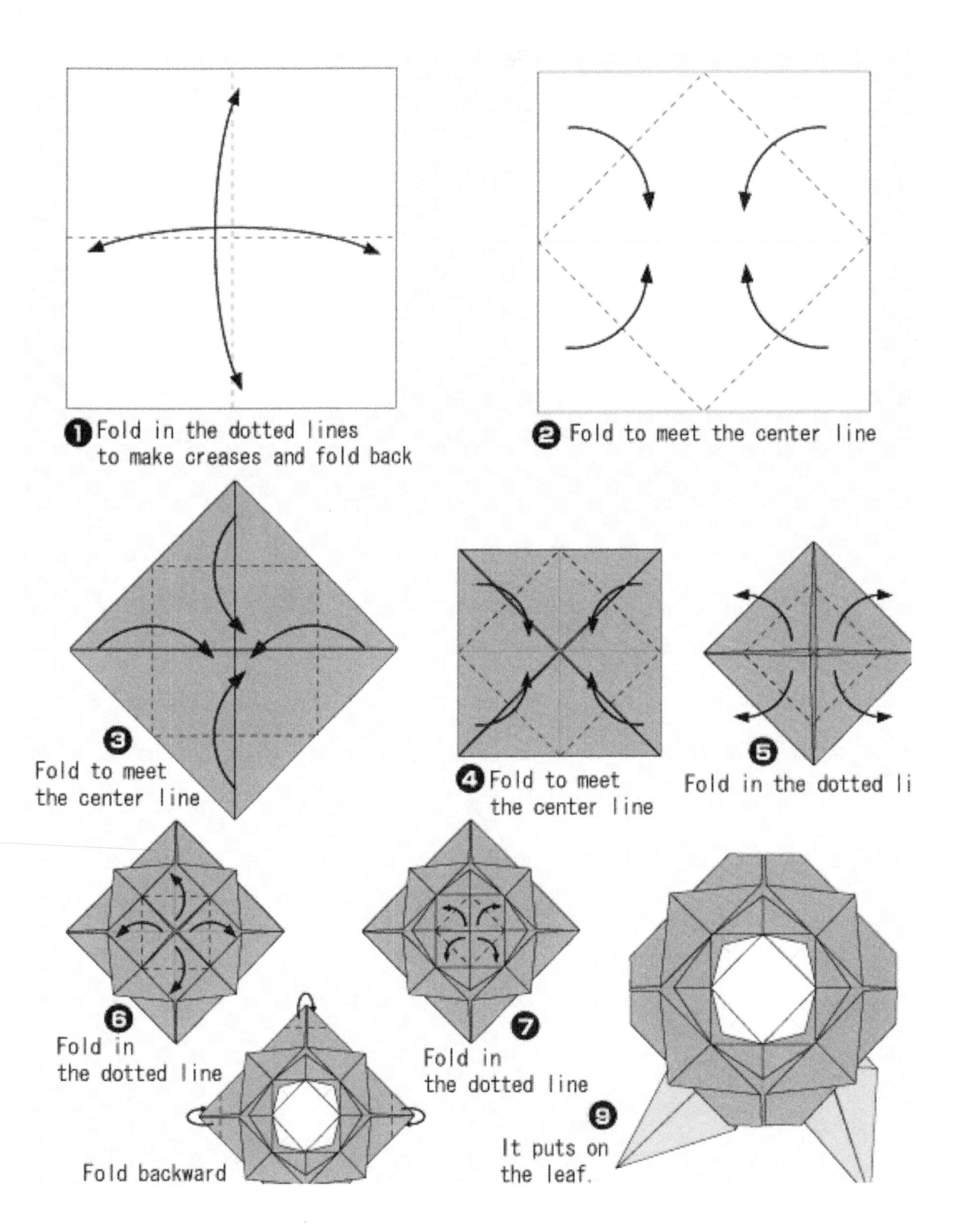

1 Fold in the dotted lines to make creases and fold back

2 Fold to meet the center line

3 Fold to meet the center line

4 Fold to meet the center line

5 Fold in the dotted li[ne]

6 Fold in the dotted line
Fold backward

7 Fold in the dotted line

9 It puts on the leaf.

40

Rose Step 1:

Fold your paper in half horizontally, unfold and then fold your paper in half vertically.

Rose Step 2:

Now fold each corner into the centre crease., fold each corner into the centre crease again, once that is done fold each corner into the centre crease for a final time.

Rose Step 3:

Next, carefully curl back all the layers of the rose. These folds should all be curled back to make the rose petals.

Rose Step 4:

To make the leaves for the rose, you need a sheet of Origami paper the same size as the paper you used for your rose. Point one point towards you and one point away from you, fold in half from point to point.

Rose Step 5:

Unfold, then fold the left and right corners into the centre crease to create a kite fold. Fold the widest corners into the centre crease once again, to create a diamond.

Rose Step 6:

Fold the diamond shape in half along the centre crease. Squash the left and right sides down, this will create the leaves.

Rose Step 7:

Flip the paper over and glue your rose to the centre of the leaves. Now you have a Rose! One of the most beautiful Origami flowers...

Once you have finished folding your rose, you could create a few more roses then bunch them together to create a very nice decoration. There are many types of roses, the rose you have just folded is the easiest... The Kawasaki Rose on the next page is a lot harder.

Kawasaki Rose (medium level)

There are many different types of Origami flowers, the Kawasaki Rose is by far the most innovative. This rose was created by a man called Toshikazu Kawasaki. The petals of this rose appear to curl around, which is why this Origami rose is very popular. This project will take a while, 50 minutes... Ask an adult for help, you will most likely need help.

Kawasaki Rose Step 1:

With the white side facing up, fold horizontally from top to bottom and unfold.

Kawasaki Rose Step 2:

Divide the paper further by folding horizontally both edges to the crease you made in the last step. Unfold – You should now have 4 rectangles down the length of your paper.

Kawasaki Rose Step 3:

Turn your paper 90° or to put it simpler, turn your paper to the right edge of your paper. Repeat steps 1-2.

Kawasaki Rose Step 4:

With the colour side up, fold the edge of the paper facing you to the 1st horizontal crease on the other side and then unfold.

Kawasaki Rose Step 5:

Repeat step 4 with each side of the paper, rotating the paper 90° each time.

Kawasaki Rose Step 6:

With the colour side still facing up, find the four centremost squares and life the horizontal plane it's on with the existing creases.

Kawasaki Rose Step 7:

Fold the four centremost squares by dividing it in half, only fold across the four centremost squares and then completely unfold.

Kawasaki Rose Step 8:

Rotate your paper 90° and repeat steps 6-7. Completely unfold once done.

Kawasaki Rose Step 9:

With the white side facing up, fold each of the four corners of your paper inwards up to the first square. Keep these corners folded in from now on!

Kawasaki Rose Step 10:

Find the centre square that is made up of two by two of the smallest squares. Reinforce the edges of that centre square with folds.

Kawasaki Rose Step 11:

Valley fold the paper diagonally in half with the white side facing up.

Kawasaki Rose Step 12:

Turn the paper 90° and repeat step 11.

Kawasaki Rose Step 13:

Turn the paper over to the colour side and fold the bottom left half only to the diagonal crease running across the centre of the paper. Fold only from the left edge to the centre, do not fold the right.

Kawasaki Rose Step 14:

Repeat step 13 three times by turning the paper 90° each time.

Kawasaki Rose Step 15:

Turn the paper over to the white side up. Valley fold left half only, from the folded-in corner nearest to you and to where the right and left edges of the fold is against the other two folded-in corners. Again, fold only from the left edge to the centre, do not fold the right.

Kawasaki Rose Step 16:

Repeat step 15 three times by turning the paper 90° each time.

Kawasaki Rose Step 17:

Fold only the right half of the nearest folded-in corner to the crease you made in step 15 and 16 so the fold is at the tip of the corner. Again, fold only from the right edge to the centre, do not fold the left.

Kawasaki Rose Step 18:

Repeat step 17 three times by turning the paper 90° each time.

Kawasaki Rose Step 19:

With the white side still facing up, fold only the left half of the nearest folded-on corner to the tip of the triangle of the folded-in corner on the opposite side. Again, only fold from the left edge to the centre, do not fold the right.

Kawasaki Rose Step 20:

Repeat step 19 three times by turning the paper 90° each time.

Kawasaki Rose Step 21:

With the white side facing up, reinforce the existing folds that lead towards the centre four small squares.

Kawasaki Rose Step 22:

Fold each of the folds you just reinforced to the right on the existing creases immediately next to it. Only fold all the way near the edges of the paper. Stay on existing crease...

Kawasaki Rose Step 23:

Check both the bottom and top of the paper to make sure you are on existing creases, if not then fix it.

Kawasaki Rose Step 24:

To form the twist, twist and flatten the centre four squares against the paper. Make sure that the crease that is under the centre crease leading to the squares is entirely folded.

Kawasaki Rose Step 25:

With the colour side facing up, pull the nearest corner open to the first existing mountain fold. Do not create any new folds.

Kawasaki Rose Step 26:

With the pulled-open part facing you, fold in the left corner along the mountain folds.

Kawasaki Rose Step 27:

With the pulled-open part still facing you, take the left corner of the square on the pulled-open part and valley fold it to the upper right corner of the square. This is a new fold, keep these folded.

Kawasaki Rose Step 28:

Repeat steps 25-27 on all the other three corners.

Kawasaki Rose Step 29:

Check the top and bottom again to make sure you are on existing creases, if not then fix it.

Kawasaki Rose Step 30:

Fold the opened-up part closest to you to the left against an existing valley fold and squeeze it there with your fingers.

Kawasaki Rose Step 31:

Fold the opened-up part to the right and over where your fingers are squeezing. Fold over the flap that is extending over to lock these two parts.

Kawasaki Rose Step 32:

Lock every single opened-up part together by repeating steps 30-31. This will be tricky, take your time and make sure to stay on existing creases.

Kawasaki Rose Step 33:

Begin closing up the bottom by folding one of the points gently into the bottom with a very gentle crease. A hard crease at this point will make the flower look unnatural - Use your fingers to keep it down.

Kawasaki Rose Step 34:

Fold the point to the left of the one you just folded on top of it and the one after that on top of them all. You should be holding them in place. One point should be sticking up still, that is fine.

Kawasaki Rose Step 35:

Tuck the last point into the first fold you folded in, while having it go over the third one you folded in. The bottom should be closed neatly now and stay closed without you holding it down.

Kawasaki Rose Step 36:

Turn your paper so that the top of the flower is on top, open up the flaps that are going into the centre.

Kawasaki Rose Step 37:

Gently pull them out from the centre and spread them, like petals. You do now want to tear anything so be careful.

Kawasaki Rose Step 38:

Using your finger smoothen the petals, make them look full and round. Ease any crumples in the paper and do your best to make the petals stay on existing creases.

Kawasaki Rose Step 39:

Pull the triangle flaps out gently on the side and curl them out slightly to make your rose look even better. Again, you don't want to rip anything…

Kawasaki Rose Step 40:

Your Kawasaki Rose is finished! Congratulations, that was very hard…

CHAPTER 3: AIRPLANES

Paper Airplanes have to be the most fun paper activity for kids! There are quite a few tricky airplanes, but most are simple to do and very fun to use when completed. Printer paper is better to use than Origami paper for paper Airplanes. In this chapter there are quite a few different paper airplanes for you to fold and test out. Don't forget to check out the Airplane game at the back of the book, using one of the airplanes from this chapter. Enjoy flying!

The simplest Airplane

Kids these days have much fancier toys than a paper airplane, but they definitely will have fun folding and flying this airplane! The easiest paper airplane to do, but still very fun to use. Many other paper airplanes have harder folds or take a longer amount of time, this simple paper airplane takes under a minute to fold... Ready to begin folding and start your piloting career? Let's go captain!

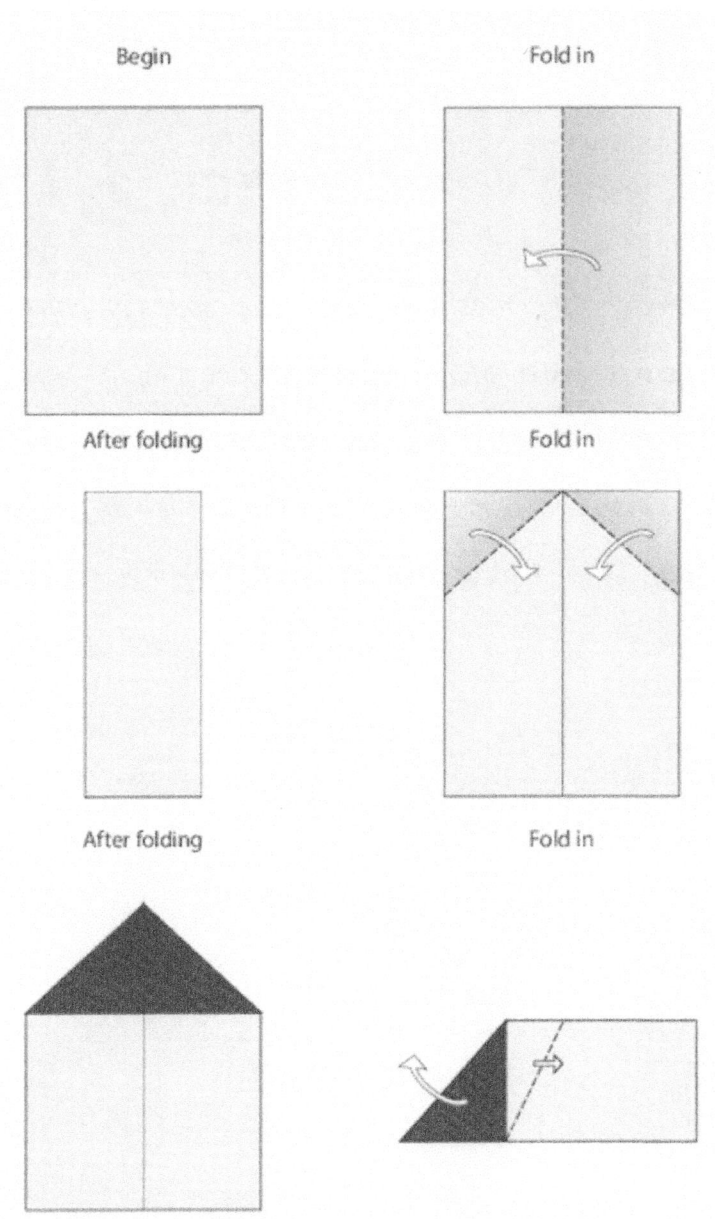

Begin

Fold in

After folding

Fold in

After folding

Fold in

The Simplest Airplane Step 1:

Fold your paper in half vertically, down the middle. Then unfold, this will create a crease.

The Simplest Airplane Step 2:

Fold the top left and top right corners towards the centre crease line. Now fold in half down the centre crease line, to from the body of the plane. Next, fold the wings down.

The Simplest Airplane Step 3:

Finally, unfold the wings from the body... Now you have the simplest airplane, wasn't that easy?

Air fighter

The air fighter is probably the most commonly folded airplane, with good reason! This paper airplane flies very well and is very easy to fold. If you want to create a greater looking paper airplane than the simplest paper airplane, then try folding the air fighter! It is just as easy to do, except this paper airplane looks a lot better and flies a lot better... Ready to fold your air fighter?

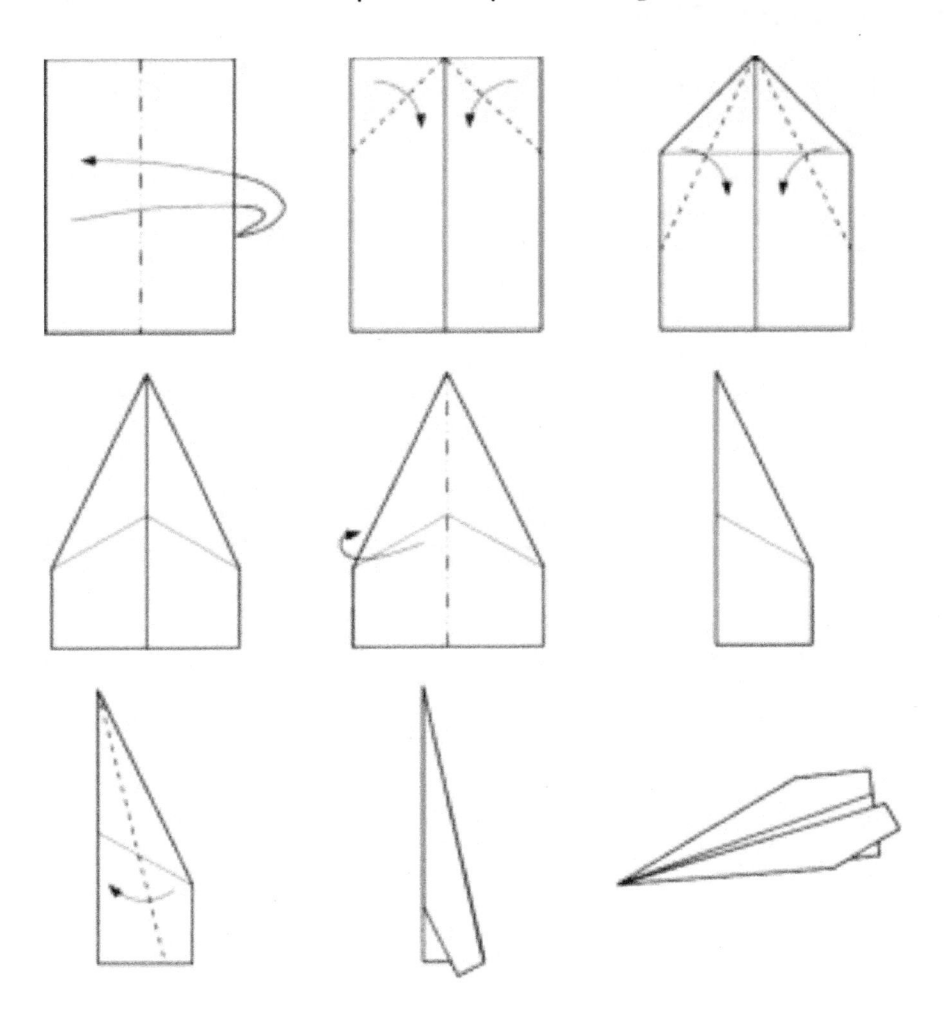

Air Fighter Step 1:

Fold your paper in half vertically, down the middle. Unfold, this will create a crease.

Air Fighter Step 2:

Next, fold the top left and top right corners towards the centre crease line. Then, fold the left and right outer corners in towards the centre crease.

Air Fighter Step 3:

Now, fold the paper in half down the centre crease line to form the body of the airplane. Fold each wing down.

Air Fighter Step 4:

Finally, unfold the wings from the body... Go fly your fighter!

High performance airplane

The high-performance paper airplane is for those of you who want to have the best flying airplane. Not only can it fly very well, it looks pretty impressive! Paper airplanes are very easy to do, some can be difficult but why fold a difficult airplane when you can fold an easy paper airplane that flies just as well... Ready to fold the plane that will be the best performing paper airplane!

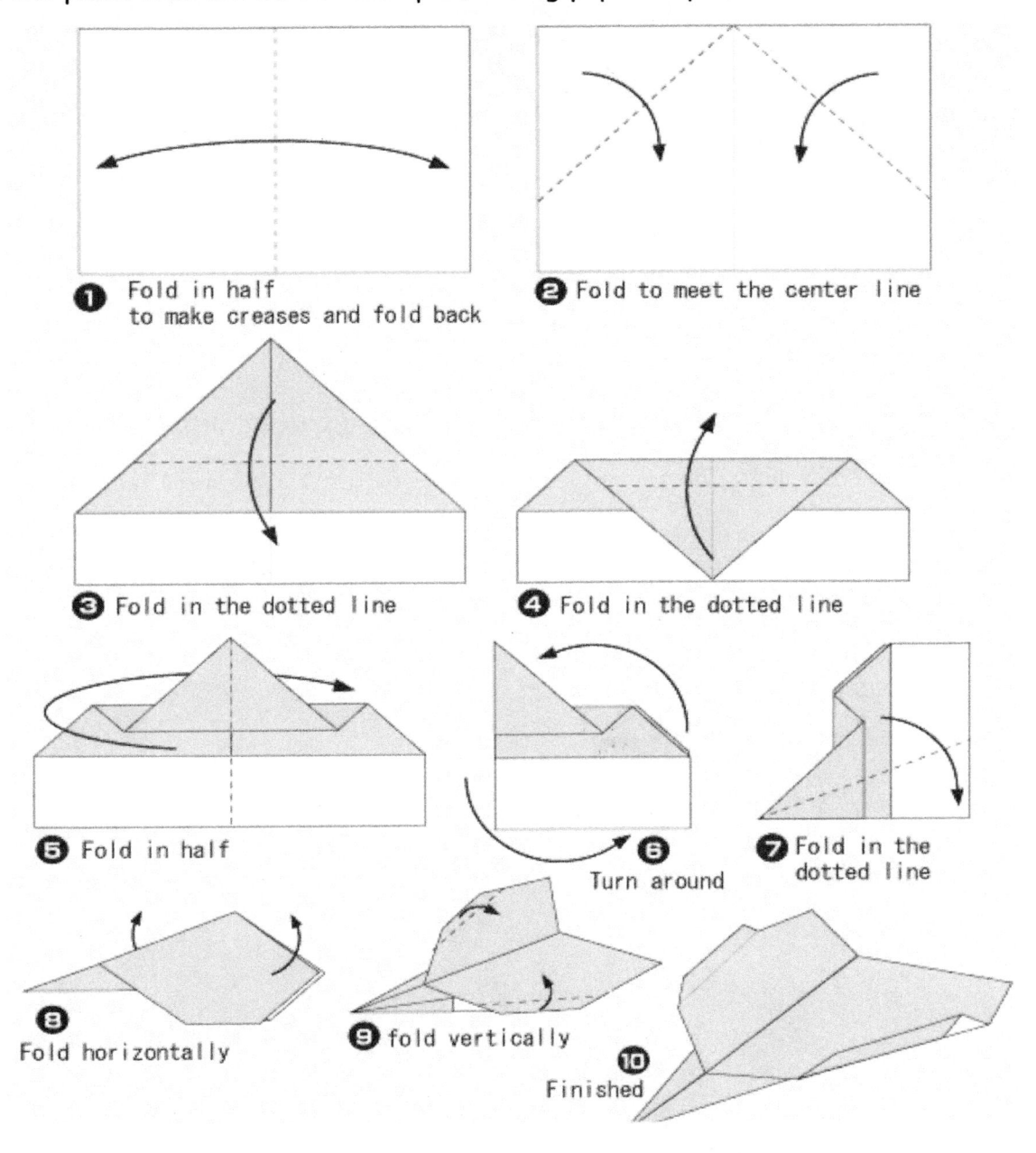

1 Fold in half to make creases and fold back

2 Fold to meet the center line

3 Fold in the dotted line

4 Fold in the dotted line

5 Fold in half

6 Turn around

7 Fold in the dotted line

8 Fold horizontally

9 fold vertically

10 Finished

High Performance Airplane Step 1:

Fold your paper in half vertically, down the middle. Unfold, this will create a crease.

High Performance Airplane Step 2:

Next, fold the top left and top right corners towards the centre crease line.

High Performance Airplane Step 3:

Now fold the top point down to the bottom edge of the paper, then fold the top left and right corners towards the centre crease line.

High Performance Airplane Step 4:

Take the top point that was folded down, fold that back over. Only fold the point that was showing back over.

High Performance Airplane Step 5:

Fold the paper in half down the centre crease line to form the body of the airplane. Fold each wing down.

High Performance Airplane Step 6:

Finally, unfold the wings from the body... Doesn't that look good? It flies even better, try it!

Airplane with landing gear

Have you folded all of the planes but feel like you want a plane with more detail? Well, then try folding the airplane with a landing gear! It may be a challenge, but once done it will look incredible. You will definitely have the most impressive looking paper airplane out of all your friends and family! Ready to attempt to fold the airplane with landing gear...

Airplane With Landing Gear Step 1:

Fold the paper in half from horizontally, from top to bottom. Unfold, this will create a crease.

Airplane With Landing Gear Step 2:

Make 3 folds, like the ones below... All of the folds pointing towards the centre. To do this, fold the top left corner across to the lower right and unfold. Then repeat the process for the top right corner.

Airplane With Landing Gear Step 3:

Push the 3 folds together, then flatten on top to create a triangular shape.

Airplane With Landing Gear Step 4:

Fold the top point back behind the paper, so that the top of the paper has a flat edge. Then fold the left and right edges of the upper flap towards the centre crease line.

Airplane With Landing Gear Step 5:

Fold the lower edges of the last 2 folds up towards the centre but keep towards the side edges.

Airplane With Landing Gear Step 6:

Fold the free corner of the two small triangular flaps down towards the edge.

Airplane With Landing Gear Step 7:

Unfold the 2 small triangular flaps to their original place but do not crease, let them lie as they are.

Airplane With Landing Gear Step 8:

This step is quite difficult. On the right-side flap that you have just folded back to the original place, you need to fold it back to the left, then fold the top triangular part of that flap down. Squash the paper down. Repeat the process for the other flap on the left side.

Airplane With Landing Gear Step 9:

Fold the paper in half along the centre crease line, then fold the landing gears down but don't crease. Fold the wings down at a slight angle.

Airplane With Landing Gear Step 10:

Fold the wings up... You now have an Airplane with a landing gear! Go impress your friends!

Swallow paper airplane

The swallow paper airplane is quite hard to do but it has been named the best paper airplane. There is no harm in trying, of course it flies very well and looks incredible so if you want a great paper airplane then this is the one for you. This is definitely the best paper airplane for flying, you may need help by an adult for this one. Ready to start folding the swallow paper airplane!

Swallow Paper Airplane Step 1:

Start with an A4 sheet of paper, valley fold the top left corner over to the right. Not all the way to the bottom, look at the image for help.

Swallow Paper Airplane Step 2:

Unfold, then repeat the process with the top right corner. In the centre of the "X", fold horizontally behind the paper. Then unfold.

Swallow Paper Airplane Step 3:

Push all the folds together and then flatten, this will create a triangular shape.

Swallow Paper Airplane Step 4:

Fold the left corner of the top flap upwards and align the corner with the top point. Repeat for the right corner of the top flap.

Swallow Paper Airplane Step 5:

Now fold the top corners of the last fold you did down and align with the bottom corner of the last fold you did. Fold the corner of the left flap towards the centre crease line, repeat for the right flap.

Swallow Paper Airplane Step 6:

Unfold the last fold you did for the 2 flaps; you need to make a squash fold next. To do this, bring the left flap towards the centre crease line then squash. Repeat for the right flap.

Swallow Paper Airplane Step 7:

Fold the bottom edge of the piece of paper up, then cut it with scissors. Ask an adult for help for this part. Then fold the top point back behind the paper, then fold the paper in half to form the body.

Swallow Paper Airplane Step 8:
Take the left wing and fold it over the right win, then unfold. Now fold the tips of the wings up at the edge.

Swallow Paper Airplane Step 9:
Go back to that strip of paper that you cut off, fold it in half lengthwise. One inch from the end cut down halfway. Do not cut it off entirely...

Swallow Paper Airplane Step 10:
Then fold down each half of the cut you just made, now insert the other end of the paper into the wing section of the airplane and push it in the entire way.

Swallow Paper Airplane Step 11:
Flip over... Your swallow paper airplane is complete! Have fun gliding that through the air, it is a great flyer.

Circular glider

The circular glider, is a very unique glider that looks like it won't fly at first glance... But, it can fly well for an oddly shaped glider. If you want to impress friends or family, or just test out something quite weird then this glider is for you! Show off to friends and family. This glider can be quite difficult to do, so once again ask an adult for help...

Circular Glider Step 1:

Start with a square piece of Origami paper, fold diagonally from point to point. Make sure to crease well.

Circular Glider Step 2:

Fold the bottom edge upwards, folding up 1cm will be enough.

Circular Glider Step 3:

Next, fold that same edge into a circle slot one end into the opening of the other end and slide it in as far as it can go.

Circular Glider Step 4:

Finally, smooth out the circle with your fingers. Now your glider is ready to fly, to fly it follow the instructions below.

How to fly it:

Hold the pointed edge between your thumb and forefinger, hold the glider in the air and watch it glide to the floor! Have fun...

CHAPTER 4: THE BEST ORIGAMI

In this chapter learn how to fold a variety of fun Origami pieces! These projects are very fun to fold and use, just make sure to try them all! You won't need the help of an adult for these, all are very simple and easy... You will enjoy them though.

Cootie catcher

An Origami Cootie Catcher is simple to make and very fun to play with! Also known as fortune tellers... Follow the step-by-step instructions to find out how to make one. You will need a square piece of paper for this. Cootie Catchers or Fortune Tellers were very popular in the 90s and early 2000s in schools. Ready to fold your Cootie Catcher and try it out on your family or friends? Follow the step-by-step instructions below...

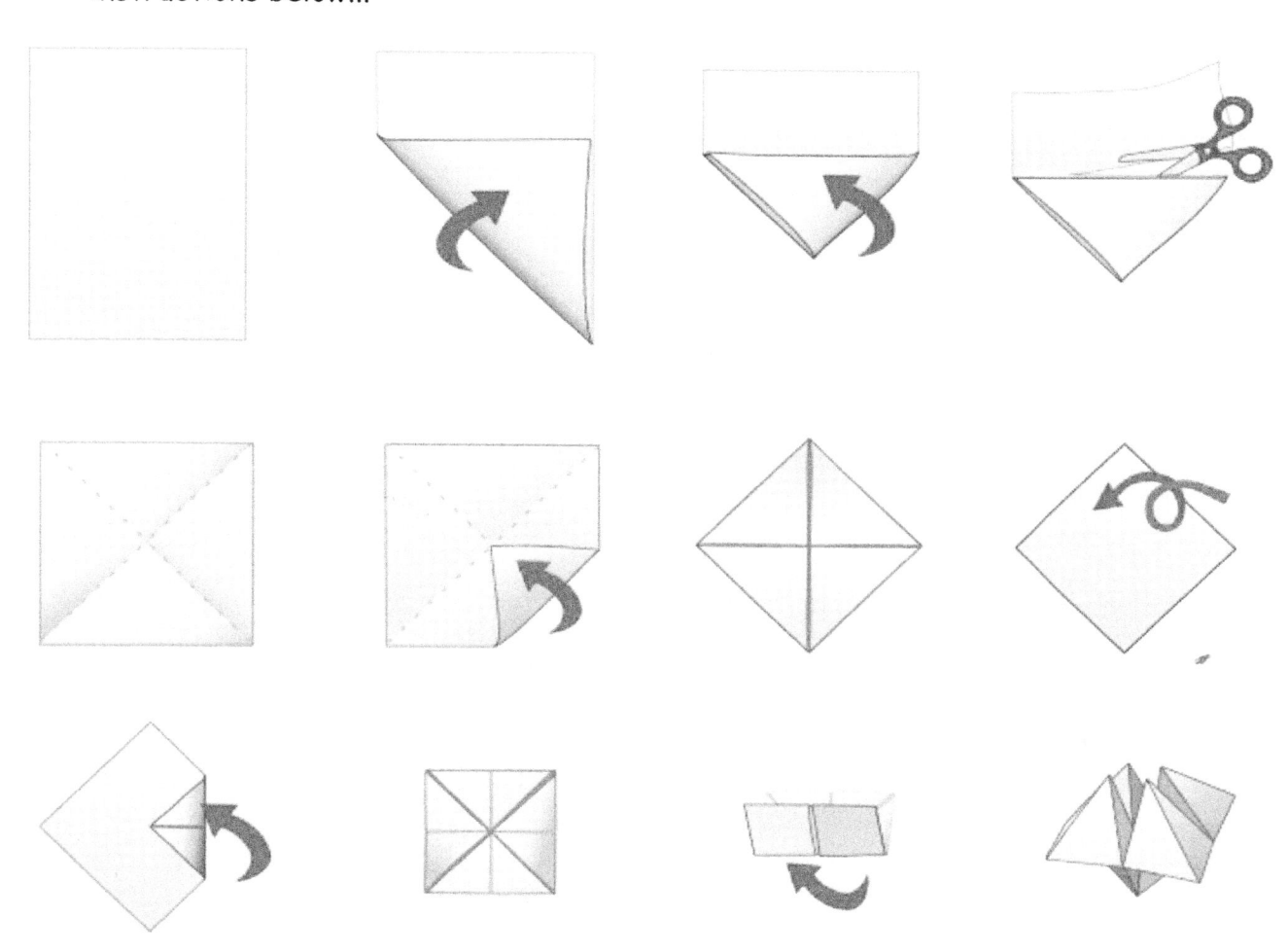

Cootie Catcher Step 1:

Begin by folding your square piece of Origami paper diagonally both ways, this will create an "X" at the centre of your paper. Now fold all of your corners into the centre point of the "X".

Cootie Catcher Step 2:

Flip the paper over and fold all the corners into the centre point of the "X" again. Then, fold the paper in half horizontally.

Cootie Catcher Step 3:

Pick the paper up and push all the points inwards, pinch the paper to the centre using your fingers.

Cootie Catcher Step 4:

Turn the paper to the side and pull out the flaps, after a bit of shaping your Cootie Catcher is ready! You should know how to play the Cootie Catcher game but if not check out our instructions on how to play the Cootie Catcher game at the end of the book!

Go to the Funny Origami Games chapter to learn how to use these once folded...

Snowflake

These Origami snowflakes are very easy and simple to make. They make very good Christmas decorations, for Christmas trees, walls, windows or greeting cards! A great activity for a family with young kids to do in the winter season. All you need is a square piece of Origami paper and some scissors. If you follow the step-by-step instructions below, you will have a snowflake ready to hang anywhere in just a few minutes...

Works best with tracing paper

Expanded view. Concentrating on one flap.

Repeat on the other 5 flaps

Full view.

Tuck this flap underneath Repeat on the other 11.

Repeat on the other 5 flaps

Repeat on the other 5 flaps

Snowflake Step 1:

Fold in half horizontally and then fold in half vertically to get crease lines. Unfold, then fold one corner to the centre of the paper, fold down the edge of that flap. This will give you two additional crease lines.

Snowflake Step 2:

Fold the paper in half again, fold down the flap from the point, do not fold the entire flap just the pointed bit. The diagram above shows what the paper should look like once you flip it over.

Snowflake Step 3:

Now fold the bigger flap on the right behind the paper, you should be left with a heart-like shape.

Snowflake Step 4:

Cut along the dotted line below, you should be left with a hexagon.

Snowflake Step 5:

Fold the edge of the hexagon towards the centre to create a crease line, repeat for all 6 edges.

Snowflake Step 6:

Fold an edge of the hexagon to the centre again, then fold the right flap over the left flap. Repeat until you get a pinwheel-like shape.

Snowflake Step 7:

Squash fold each flap pocket, on each of these flattened pockets fold the edges closest to the centre towards the centre crease of each pocket.

Snowflake Step 8:

Unfold the squash folds to reveal the crease lines, for each of the pockets fold the point closest to the centre towards the outermost point.

Snowflake Step 9:

Turn the paper over, bring each pointed tip of the hexagon towards the centre. Each fold will expose a tiny flap, do not hide this fold underneath.

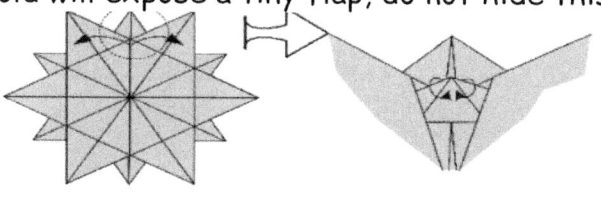

Open out slightly as marked

Bring the two flaps to the front.

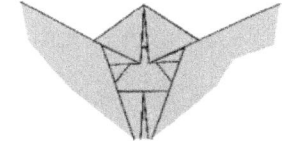

Repeat on the other five similar areas

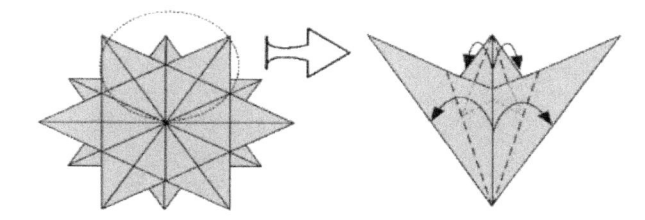

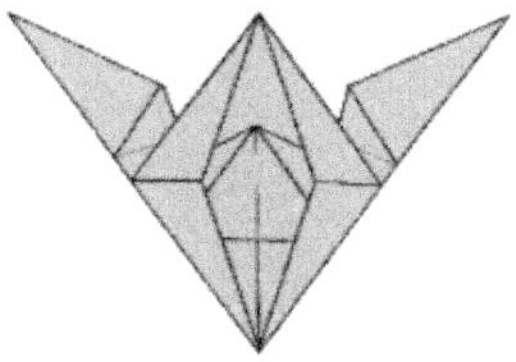

Repeat on the other five similar areas

Finished.

This is an attempt to see the effect of multiple layers of tracing paper

Snowflake Step 10:

Squash fold each of the tiny flaps. Invert the folds done in the last step, neatly hiding the flaps underneath.

Snowflake Step 11:

Flip the paper over, bring each tip from the centre as far out as possible and fold. You should be left with 12 flaps – 6 big flaps and 6 small flaps.

Snowflake Step 12:

Flip the paper over again, in between the big flaps is a small flap. Move forward each of the small flaps, once done you should have 6 kite-like shapes.

Snowflake Step 13:

For each half of a "kite" bring the lower left edge to the centre crease of the "kite", squash the pop up towards the edge. Do this for each one... Once done, your snowflake is complete! Hang them anywhere you like.

Cute origami Santa

Origami Santa's are a great project for kids near Christmas. This Origami project can be really easy if you follow the step-by-step instructions below! All you need is a square sheet of Origami paper, preferably use paper that is red on one side and white on the other. You will need an adult to help with this... Are you ready to fold Santa Clause? The better you fold, the more gifts he sends you.

Cute Origami Santa Step 1:

Start with your paper colour side up. Fold your paper from top to bottom and then from left to right. Flip the paper over and fold the bottom edge to meet the horizontal crease and unfold.

Cute Origami Santa Step 2:

Fold the left edge to meet the vertical centre crease line and unfold, fold the bottom right corner up to the top left corner and unfold.

Cute Origami Santa Step 3:

Turn the paper so that the diagonal line is vertically centred and flip the paper to the over side.

Cute Origami Santa Step 4:

Fold the bottom corner up to just below the centre and unfold. Then fold the corner to the previous crease line and then unfold.

Cute Origami Santa Step 5:

Next, fold the bottom corner up to the crease you just made and then unfold. Fold the bottom corner up to the last crease line you made. Fold the bottom section up, fold the bottom section up again and fold the bottom section up one last time.

Cute Origami Santa Step 6:

Turn the paper over to the other side, turn the paper so that the folded corner is now at the top. Unfold the paper.

Cute Origami Santa Step 7:

Bring the top left and top right sections in towards the centre, squash the top section down and fold well. Now, fold the bottom corner up to the top corner, this will create a triangle.

Cute Origami Santa Step 8:

Fold the top corner down of the top piece of paper, leaving a small gap between Santa's beard and his hat. Fold another small section down creating Santa's beard.

Cute Origami Santa Step 9:

Flip the paper to the other side, fold the bottom right corner up to the top corner. Fold the bottom left corner to the top corner.

Step 10:

Now, fold the right side to the center, make sure to fold all the layers. Repeat for the left side. Fold the bottom corner up a little bit.

Cute Origami Santa Step 11:

Your Santa is now complete! Decorate him so that he looks like Santa... Have fun with this Christmas decoration.

Once you have folded your Santa, color him... Then there are many different things you can use your little Santa for. As a decoration, on a Christmas card, hung up on a Christmas tree, on a table or stuck on a present for a great wrapping addition.

Easy leaves

These leaves make great decorations all year round, there are many ways you can use Origami leaves. A nice Origami activity for kids would be to paint them once they are completed to create different coloured leaves. Origami leaves are very easy to do and look very pretty when done, a good activity for a family or young student at school...

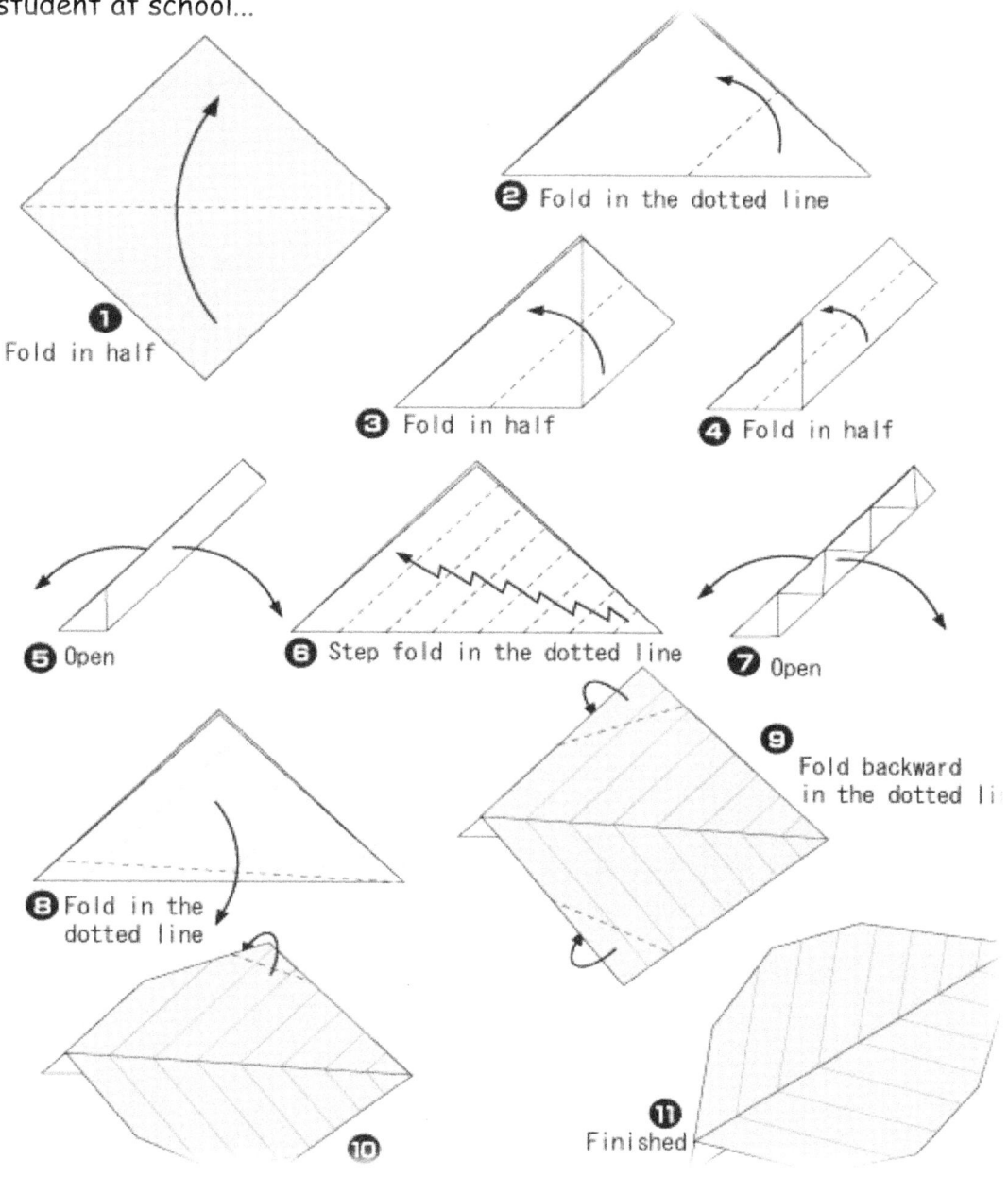

❶ Fold in half

❷ Fold in the dotted line

❸ Fold in half

❹ Fold in half

❺ Open

❻ Step fold in the dotted line

❼ Open

❽ Fold in the dotted line

❾ Fold backward in the dotted li

❿

⓫ Finished

Easy Leaves Step 1:

Begin with your paper colour side facing up, this colour/pattern will be the colour of the leaf. Fold your paper in half bringing the top left corner down to the bottom right corner and crease well.

Easy Leaves Step 2:

Next, make another crease, starting from the top point, down to the bottom right point. The section should become bigger towards the left.

Easy Leaves Step 3:

Flip your paper over so that it is going from left to right, with the crease you just did in the bottom right corner. Fold the top point down to the bottom left corner, creasing well. Unfold.

Easy Leaves Step 4:

Next, fold the top point and bottom point to the crease line you have just made. Flip the paper back over to the other side.

Easy Leaves Step 5:

Bring the bottom edge up to the top first crease, then unfold. Bring the top point to the bottom first crease. Next, fold the top and bottom to the nearest crease.

Easy Leaves Step 6:

Fold the bottom right corner of the top layer inwards, aligning with the third horizontal crease from the bottom.

Easy Leaves Step 7:

Fold the edges of last fold to make the lead edge. Flip over and repeat on the other side.

Easy Leaves Step 8:

Open the leaf, now you have a leaf! Wasn't that easy...

Once you have folded your easy leaf, paint it to make it look that little bit better... After that you can use your leaf all your round, as a decoration – Hung up, on a window, front of a notebook, on your bedroom door, for a birthday or celebration card. So many possibilities, it is your choice what you use this leaf for... After all, you made it!

Star boxes

This beautiful box is perfect for storing items, such as jewellery or money... Even placing snacks in there. Perfect for Christmas or Easter! But this box is good all year round. To do this box you need a sheet of square Origami paper. Are you ready to fold this pretty little box? Follow the step-by-step instructions below...

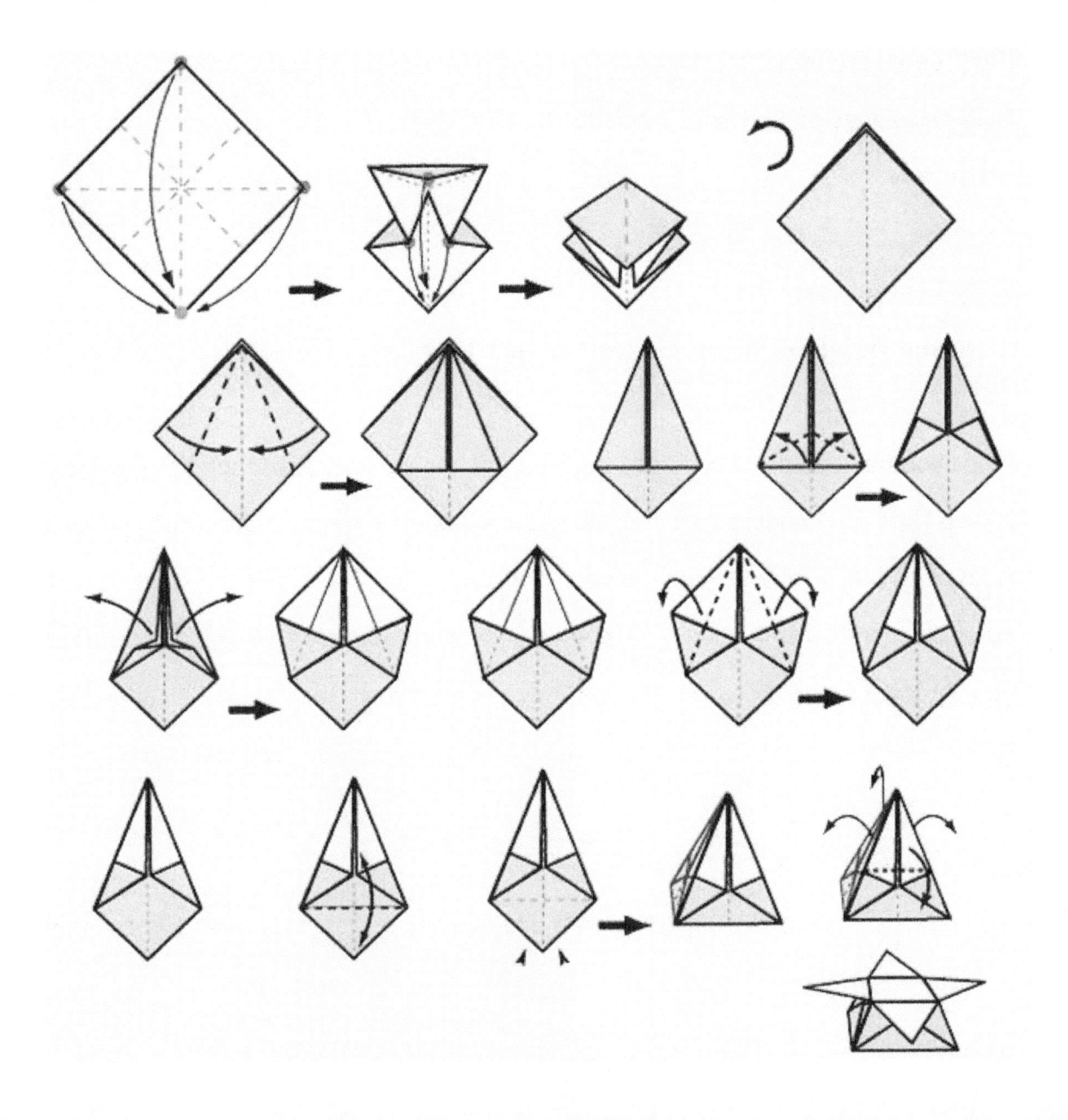

Star Boxes Step 1:

Begin with the white said facing up, fold your paper in half from left to right and from bottom to top. Flip the paper over and fold in half diagonally both ways.

Star Boxes Step 2:

Now, pick up the paper folding it in half pushing the diagonal folds into the centre of the paper.

Star Boxes Step 3:

With your square base upside down, fold the right edge to the centre crease. Repeat for the left edge.

Star Boxes Step 4:

Open the right flap that you just folded and flatten down, repeat for the left flap. Fold the right side of the flattened flap behind, repeat for the left flap. Now repeat this entire step for the other side of the paper.

Star Boxes Step 5:

Fold the bottom point up and unfold, fold one layer of the top point down. Repeat the last step for the other sides. So, fold one layer down for each side.

Star Boxes Step 6:

Open out the box carefully, do this by pulling the flaps. Now, push the bottom upwards and straighten out the edges. You should know have a very beautiful Origami box! Enjoy using the box...

Once you have folded your star box, paint it or customise it as much as you want... Then use it to store items or use as a snack holder. Either way, you can impress friends and family with this! Be careful with it though, a lot of effort went into it so don't put too much pressure on your star box.

Easy fish

If you go to the A Basic Fish section in Chapter 1 step-by-step instruction you can see one type of fish. Below is another type of fish, this fish is very easy to do. The fish below is simple to make, a few hard parts but for the most part is very easy to make. Would you like to learn how to fold another fish? Follow the steps below to have your very own Origami Fish!

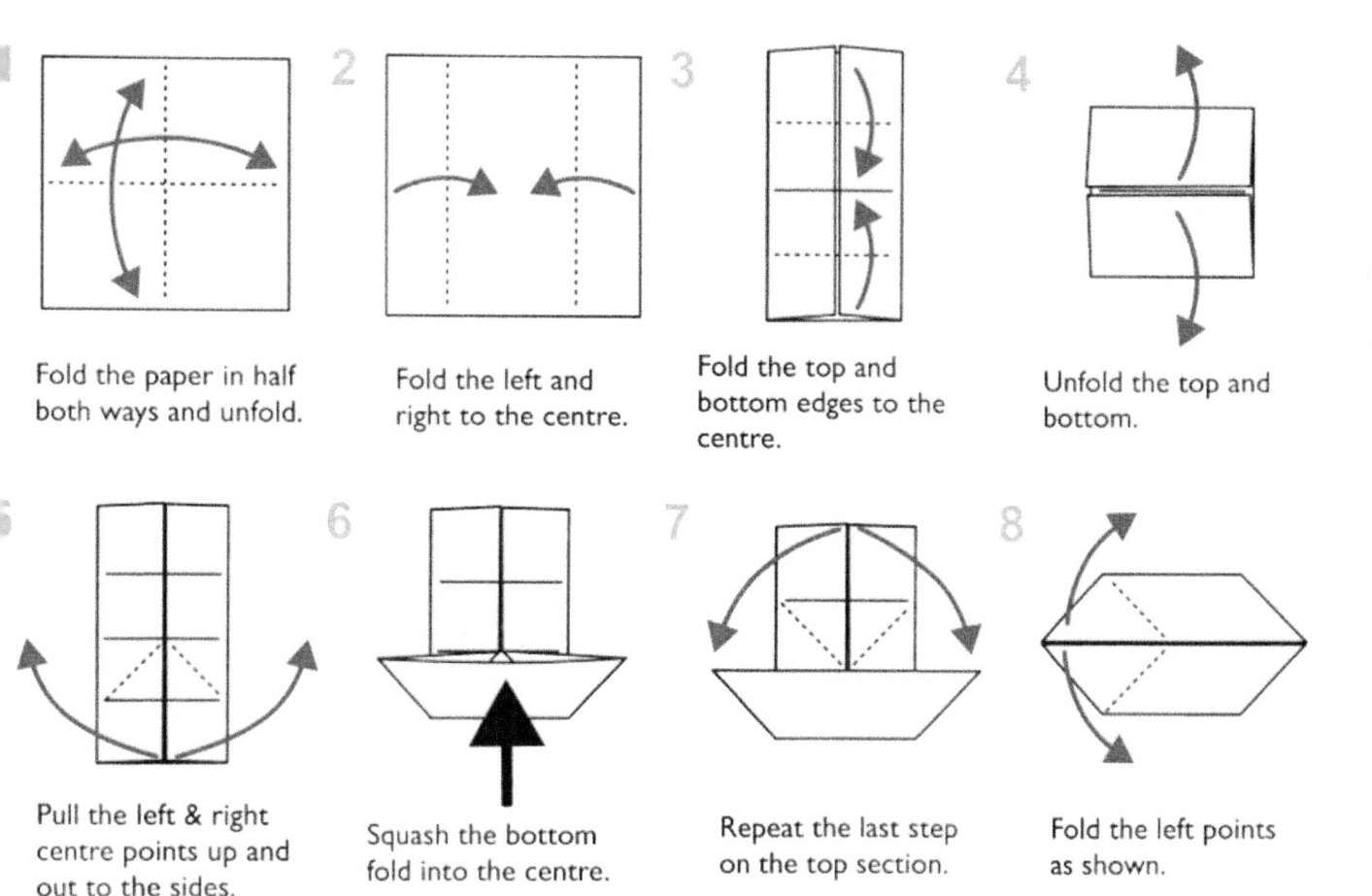

1 Fold the paper in half both ways and unfold.

2 Fold the left and right to the centre.

3 Fold the top and bottom edges to the centre.

4 Unfold the top and bottom.

5 Pull the left & right centre points up and out to the sides.

6 Squash the bottom fold into the centre.

7 Repeat the last step on the top section.

8 Fold the left points as shown.

An Easy Fish Step 1:

Fold the paper in half both ways and unfold.

An Easy Fish Step 2:

Fold the left and right to the centre, fold the top and bottom edges to the centre.

An Easy Fish Step 3:

Unfold the top and bottom, pull the left and right centre points up and out to the sides.

An Easy Fish Step 4:

Squash the bottom fold into the centre. Repeat the last step on the top section, fold the two left points as shown above.

9 Fold the corner with a green dot up to the red dot.

10 Fold the flap down from the centre.

11 Fold the corner with a green dot down to the red dot.

12 Fold the flap up from the centre.

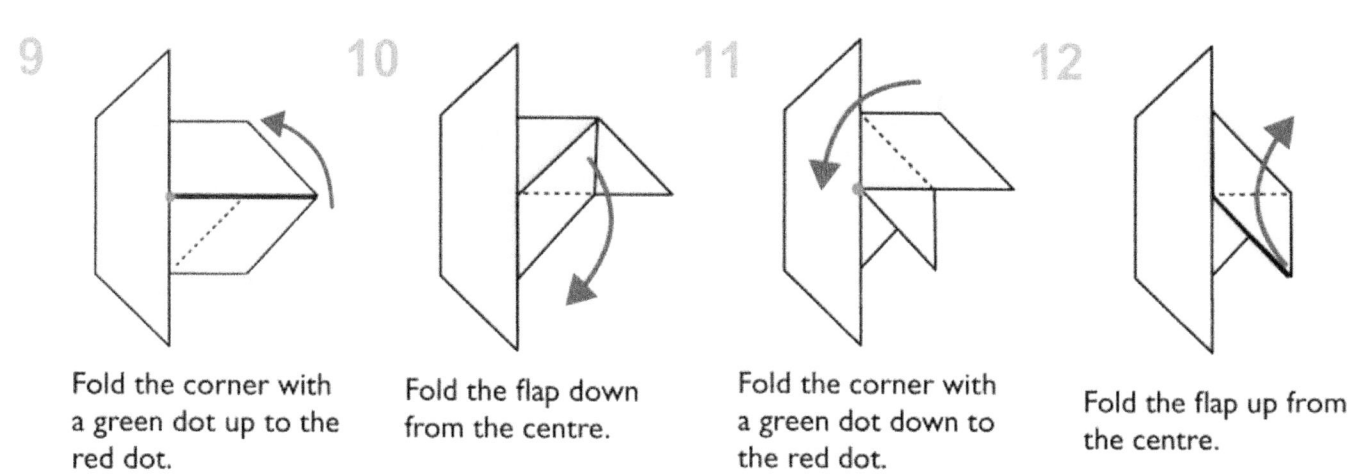

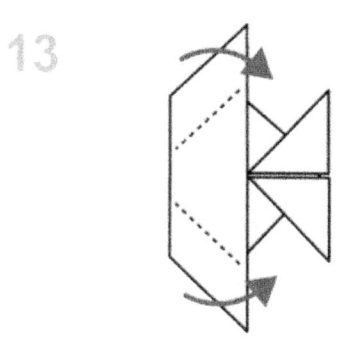

13 Fold the top & bottom corners to the right as shown.

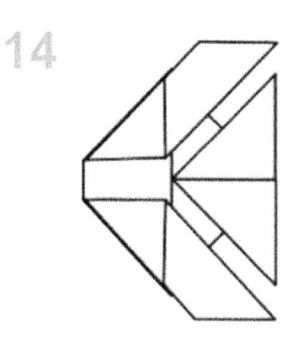

14 It should look something like this!

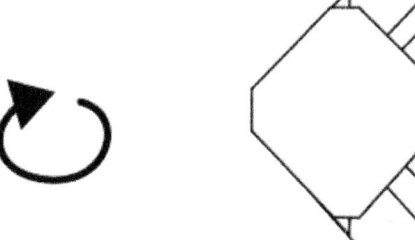

15 Turn the model to the other side.

An Easy Fish Step 5:

Fold the corner with the small dot from the bottom right corner up to the small dot on the centre fold.

An Easy Fish Step 6:

Fold the flap down from the centre, fold the corner with the small dot on the far top right in the above image down to the small dot near the centre fold.

An Easy Fish Step 7:

Fold the flap up from the centre, fold the top and bottoms corners to the right as shown above.

85

An Easy Fish Step 8:

Turn the model to the other side.

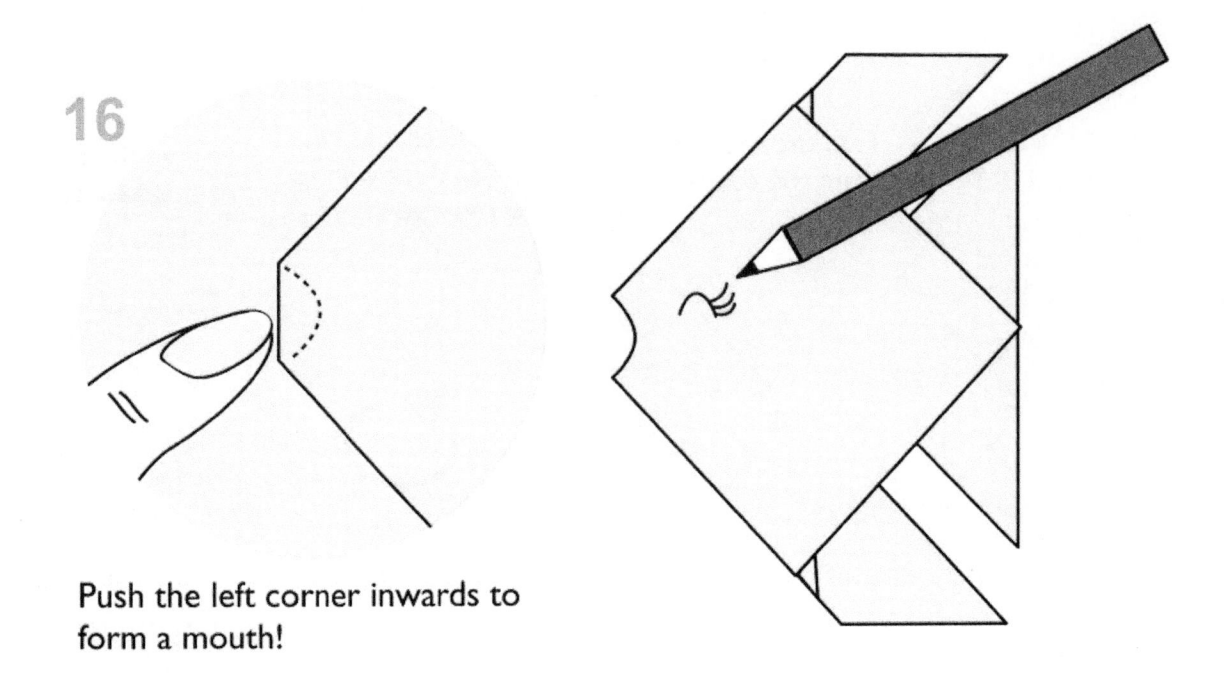

Push the left corner inwards to form a mouth!

An Easy Fish Step 9:

Push the left corner inwards to form a mouth. Add a fisheye and colour if you wish, now your easy fish is done!

Colour your fish, add scales and an eye. Once that is done you can attach it to a piece of string and hang anywhere you like! Try different sized pieces of paper for a challenge and a bit of variety. A good way to add scales is to take a ruler and draw lines across the fish, then turn the fish around and drawn lines through the lines you have just drawn. Now colour them aby colour you want...

CHAPTER 5: FUNNY ORIGAMI GAMES

Now that you have learnt how to fold, maybe you want to learn how to play some games with what you have learnt! In this chapter, you can learn how to play various different Origami games. These games are great for kids, families and school classes. You may already know some of these games, but you might not have known it was Origami. All you need to play these games are a piece of paper and a friend or family member. Some of these games have the instructions on how to fold the Origami needed in one of the chapters in this book, others have tutorials! Also, make sure to have an adult present for some of these as there are a couple that can be difficult to fold – Once folded you will have a lot of fun though...

Fortune teller

Fortune Teller was a paper game very popular in the 90s and early 2000s amongst school children. You should know how to fold a Fortune Teller since it was in the book, if not go to Cootie Catcher and learn how! The way you play Fortune Teller, is by adding colours and numbers on the different flaps of the paper Fortune Teller. Starting with colours and then numbers, after that the bottom layer of flaps needs to be filled with good and bad fortunes. After you have asked a friend for a colour, you spell out that colour and open and shut the Fortune Teller. After that, you ask for a number and then you open that flap and read out the fortune... It is that easy! Try it on a friend or family member.

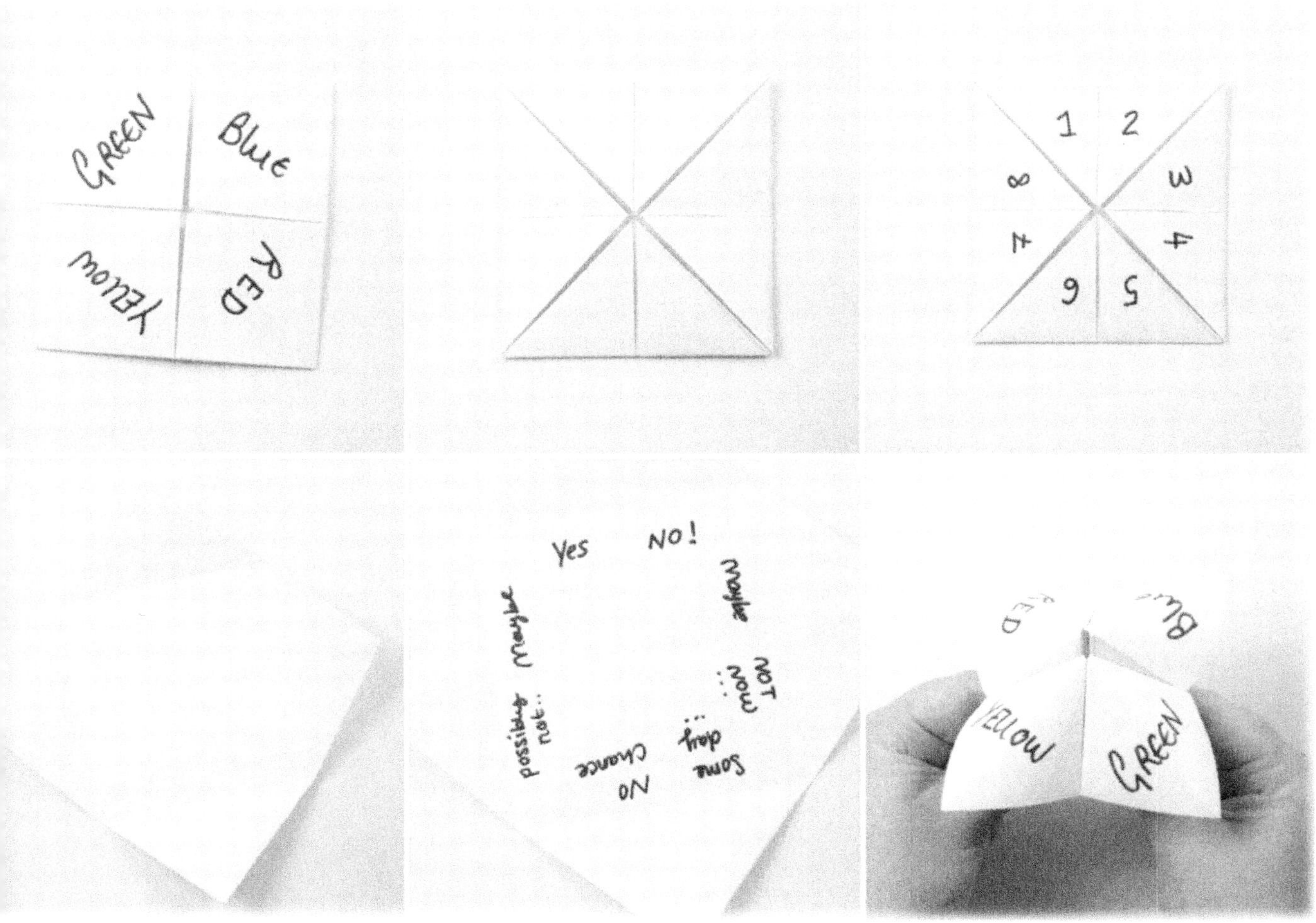
GREEN
Blue
YELLOW
RED
1
2
3
4
5
6
7
8
Yes
NO!
Maybe
NOT now..
Some day..
NO chance
possibly not..
Maybe
RED
Blue
YELLOW
GREEN

Jumping frog

Below are instructions on how to fold a Jumping Frog, once folded you can then make it jump by pressing its lower back... This frog can be folded in under 5 minutes. Have fun folding and enjoy jumping your frog around. Hop to it!

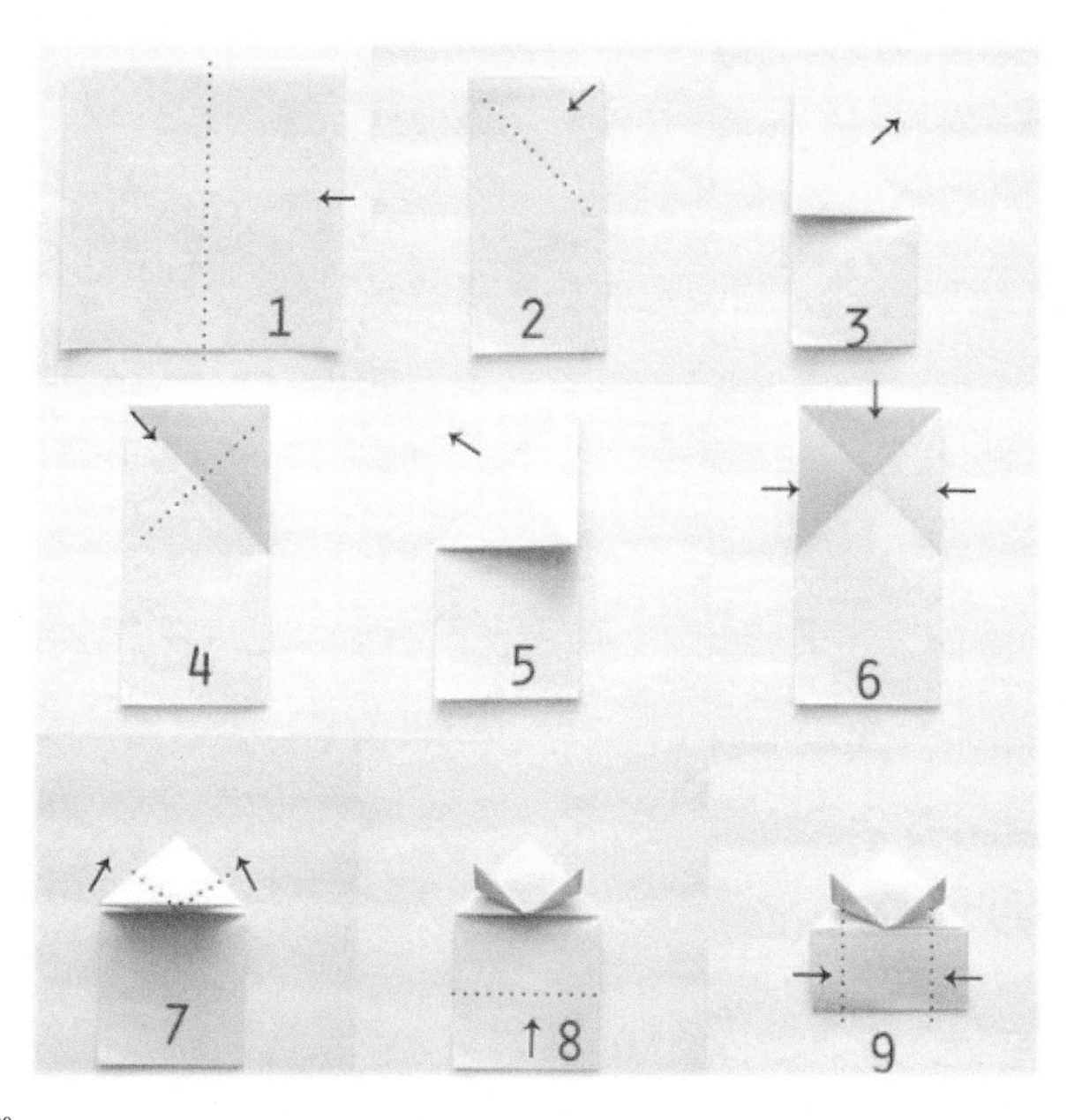

Jumping Frog Step 1:

Fold your paper in half vertically, then fold the top right corner down across to the left edge of the paper. Unfold. Repeat for the left corner. Now, pinch all corners and squash fold to create a triangle at the top of your paper. Lift the bottom edges up for the upper flap, then fold the bottom edge of your paper up. Fold your paper down.

Jumping Frog Step 2:

Fold your paper in half horizontally, now fold the left and right corners of the bottom inwards and down. Pull the 2 flaps out, now unfold those flaps down. Fold your paper in half horizontally, then fold the lower part of your paper in half again. Flip over... Now you have your frog!

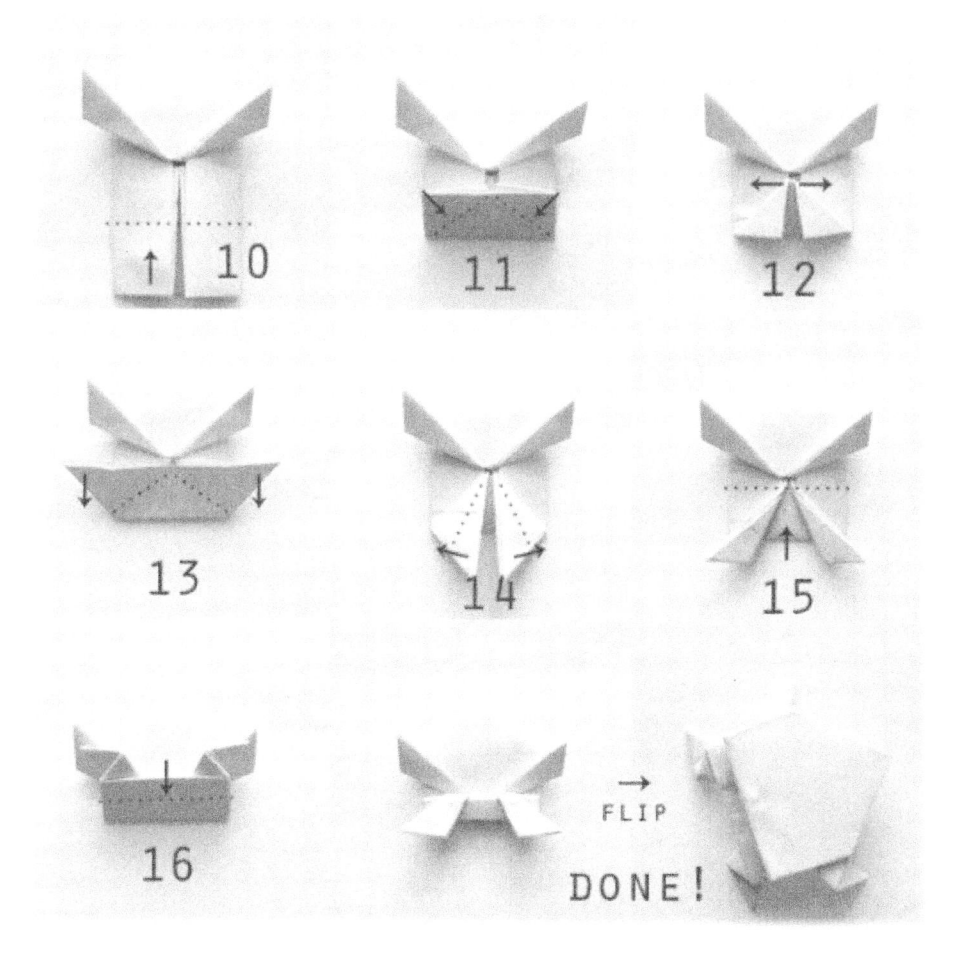

Paper airplane

For this game, take one of the airplanes from Chapter 3 and get a friend or family member to see who can throw their plane the furthest! This is a very fun game to play with family members. There is not really much to explain for this, just throw your airplane and see how far it goes...

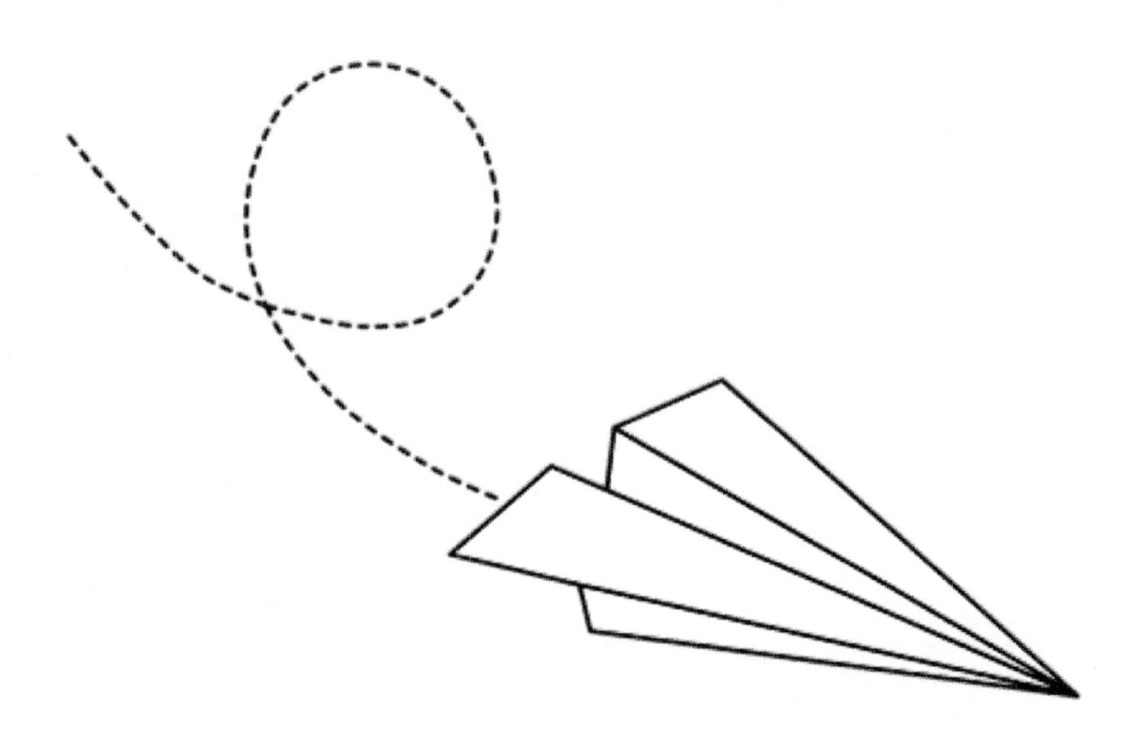

Paper basketball

Paper Basketball is actually quite simple to do, fold a Star Box, go to our tutorial for how to create Star Boxes. All that is left to do is to cut of a thin strip of paper and roll it into a ball, then find a friend or family member and see who can get the ball in the most amount of times. Another alternative for this game is to follow our instructions below on how to fold a basketball hoop and play the game that way. Young kids will enjoy folding this basketball hoop and playing with it once it is done.

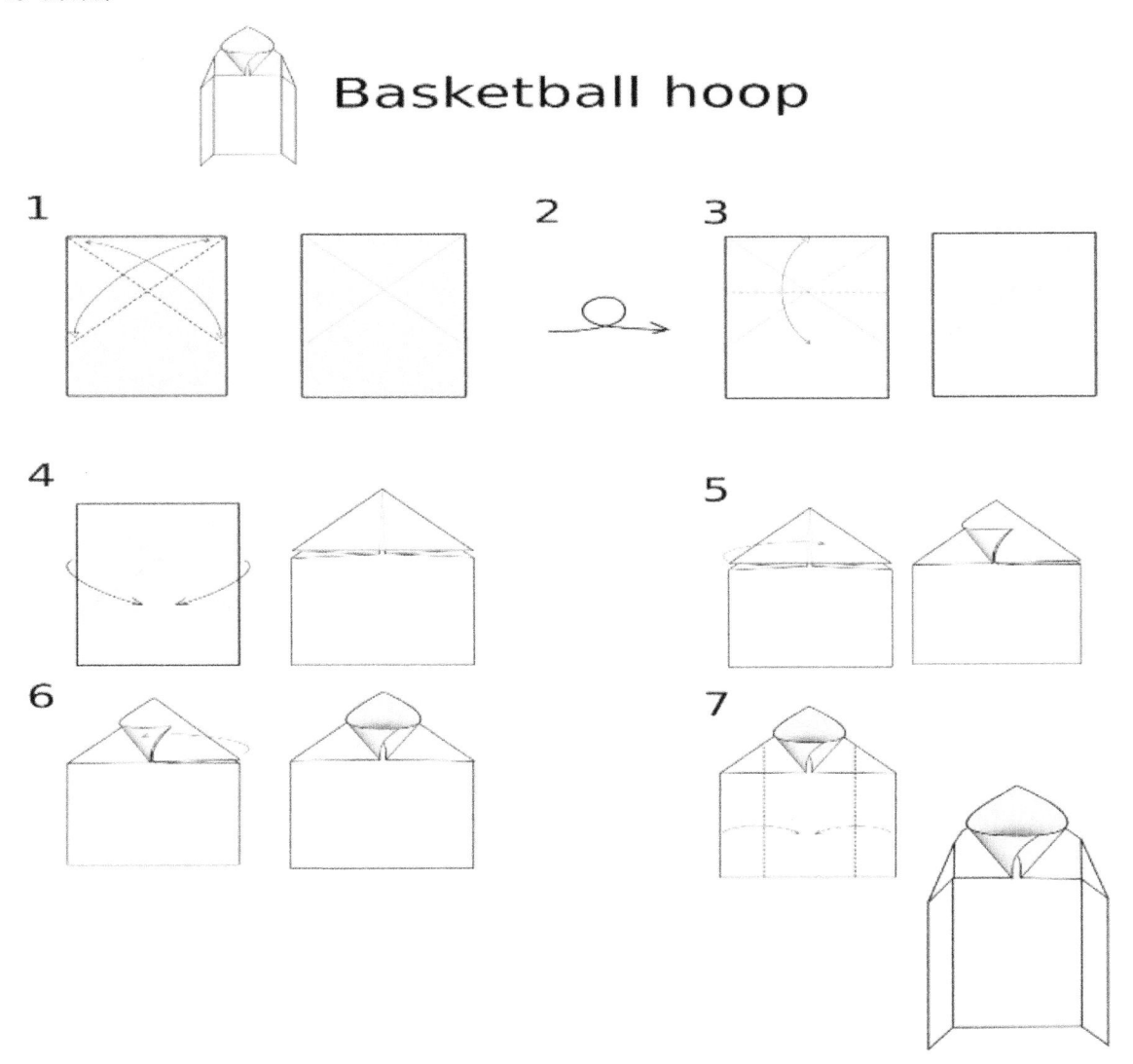

Basketball hoop

1.
2.
3.
4.
5.
6.
7.

Paper Basketball Step 1:

Use an A4 piece of paper for this. Fold the left corner diagonally over to the right edge of the paper, crease well. Unfold and then fold the right corner diagonally over to the left edge of the paper, crease well.

Paper Basketball Step 2:

Turn the paper over to the other side, now fold the paper to meet the crease halfway down and align the creases. Unfold and turn the paper over again, push the middle of the "X" down and pull the sides in. Then squash fold that which should create a triangle at the top of your paper.

Paper Basketball Step 3:

Tuck one of the corners into the other corner, this creates the hoop. Fold both outer edges to the centre crease, then open the sides... Now stand your hoop somewhere, make a paper ball and have fun!

Paper football

Most kids must have flicked a piece of paper across a table or tried to score past a friend at some point. Well, you can turn that into a game... This game is perfect for younger kids to play with family or friends, all you need is a piece of paper. Ready to begin your paper football career?

English Paper Football:

All you need to do for this is cut a thin strip of paper, scrunch that into a ball and either make goal posts with your arms and try to flick it past your friend or family member. Or you can cut 2 more thin strips of paper and place them on either side to create a makeshift goal... There is no need to fold for this game, it is a simple but fun game for all ages!

Once folded just get a friend or family member and see who can score the most goals... May the best win!

American paper football

For American Paper Football you do need to do a bit of folding but follow the diagram above and the instructions below to get an American Paper Football.

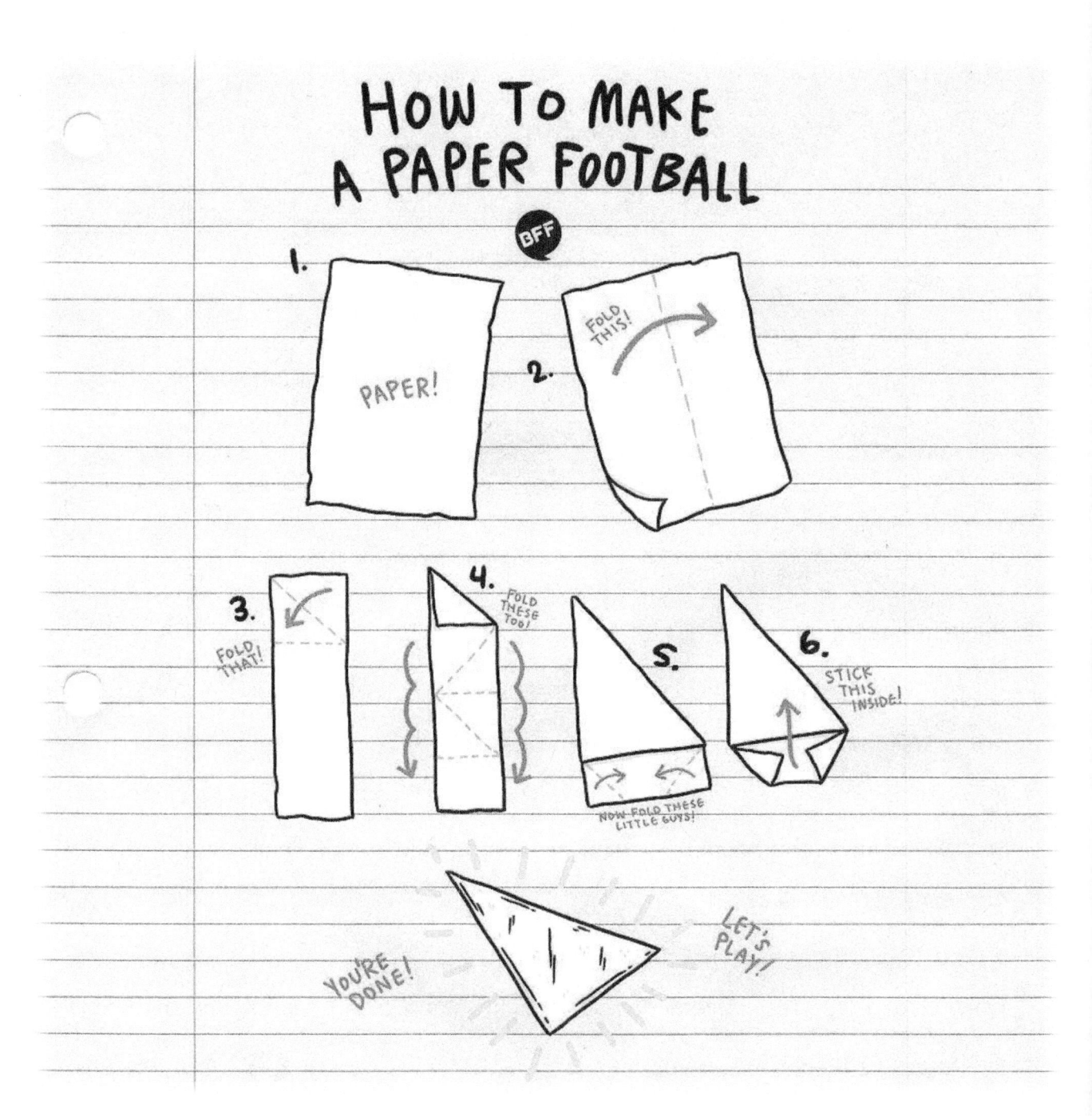

American Paper Football Step 1:

Fold your A4 paper in half from left to right, then fold the top right corner down to the dashed line.

American Paper Football Step 2:

Fold along the dashed lines in step 4 of the diagram, once that is done fold the bottom corners inwards. Then stick the flap inside and you have an American Paper Football! Enjoy...

Just find a friend or a family member and see who can get the most touchdowns! May the best win...

Final Words

Hopefully, if you are reading this then it means you have folded everything in this book! If that is the case then congratulations, you must have had a lot of fun! The Origami projects in this book were mostly aimed at children, young children, however if you have read this as a beginner then that is absolutely fine. Origami is very hard to learn, so getting this far is very good. All the things that you have learnt in this book can be used to master Origami if you wanted to... Mountain folds, valley folds, flaps, the Kawasaki Rose is very hard to learn so if you have managed to successfully fold that flower then you will most definitely be able to attempt harder Origami projects.

Thank You For Reading This Book,
Hopefully You Have Enjoyed A Lot!

Copyright © 2019
Joel Kit & John Dover
All rights reserved.

Printed in Great Britain
by Amazon